TEACHER EDUCATION IN THE PEOPLE'S REPUBLIC OF CHINA

by Rhea A. Ashmore
and Zhen Cao

Phi Delta Kappa
International Studies in Education

We can only see in a picture what our experience permits us to see.

Edgar Dale

The Phi Delta Kappa International Studies in Education Series was established as a way to enlarge the common experience of education by publishing studies that bring to readers knowledge of heretofore unfamiliar theories, philosophies, and practices in the profession of education.

As the interdependence of nations becomes increasingly evident and necessary with the passage of time, so too must our understandings about education become shared property. In thus sharing, we come increasingly to comprehend one another across civilizations and cultures, for education is at the core of human endeavor. Through education we pass on to succeeding generations not merely the accumulated wisdom of our past but the vision and means to create the future.

Teacher Education in the People's Republic of China is the second monograph in this series.

Previous title:
Elementary Teacher Education in Korea

TEACHER EDUCATION IN THE PEOPLE'S REPUBLIC OF CHINA

by Rhea A. Ashmore
and Zhen Cao

PHI DELTA KAPPA
EDUCATIONAL FOUNDATION
Bloomington, Indiana
U.S.A.

Cover design by
Peg Caudell

Library of Congress Catalog Card Number 96-70382
ISBN 0-87367-494-4
Copyright ©1997 by Rhea A. Ashmore and Zhen Cao
Phi Delta Kappa Educational Foundation
Bloomington, Indiana U.S.A.

To my father,
LeRoy C. Jones

To my grandmother,
Song Yunxian

ACKNOWLEDGMENTS

From January to July 1994, Rhea Ashmore represented the University of Montana as the faculty exchange scholar to Shanghai International Studies University (SISU) in the People's Republic of China. Thanks to the support from these institutions, she had the opportunity to live, travel, and teach in China. Furthermore, she enriched her life by making Chinese acquaintances — faculty, students, and citizens — including her Chinese co-author, Zhen Cao, who initially taught her the Chinese language.

Jihua Zhou, Zhen Cao's wife and a former high school teacher and university instructor in China, shared astute ideas for inclusion in the manuscript. Also, Yuchen Cao and Xinzhen Wang, Cao's daughter and mother, strongly supported the authors during the development of this work.

Donovan R. Walling, editor of Special Publications at Phi Delta Kappa International, promoted the manuscript and encouraged the authors to proceed with the project.

Yanbing Tang, Tianhong Yu, Ruihua Li, and Zhongyang Feng, international scholars and exchange students from the People's Republic of China, provided firsthand information and translated Chinese documents for inclusion in the manuscript.

Jodi Moreau generously assisted with graphics production.

The authors salute the individuals and institutions cited above. Their support, advice, and assistance contributed to the publication of this book.

TABLE OF CONTENTS

INTRODUCTION

To the Westerner, trying to understand China is a bit like being Alice in Wonderland: Everything strikes one as being "curiouser and curiouser." Thus to crack open the door to understanding — if not of the whole of Chinese culture, at least of China's approach to teacher education — it first is necessary to summarize the relationship between government and education in the People's Republic.

The Chinese government is a hierarchical one. The highest government authority resides in the Standing Committee of the Communist Party Politburo. The Politburo is composed of 25 members. At the next level is the 210-member Central Committee, consisting of party members and provincial party leaders. Authority is exercised by the party representatives, who are responsible to the party officials ranked above them.

Implementation of decisions made by the Politburo — the daily running of the country — rests with the State Council. The council is composed of the premier and four vice-premiers, 10 state councilors, a secretary-general, 45 ministers, and heads of various agencies.

Formerly the Ministry of Education, the State Education Commission (SEDC), a multi-functional executive branch of the State Council, is the supreme administrative authority for the education system in China. The SEDC formulates major educational policies, designs overall strategies for promoting education, coordinates educational undertakings supervised by various ministries, and directs education reform. "In short, it [SEDC] is responsible for turning out personnel well-educated and well-trained in various subjects and fields — with high standards of moral integrity, intellectual, physical and aesthetical developments — for the cause of socialist construction" (SEDC 1989, p. 36).

Since the late 1970s, the central government has focused on education reform as one of the key components to achieve the goal of the four modernizations — agriculture, industry, science and technology, and defense. Reform outlines and government mandates have significantly affected education at all levels. Chapters 1 through 3 — Past, Present, and Future — present a brief chronology of education highlights and how teacher education has evolved since the time of Confucius.

To put a human face on this evolution, we have included a number of vignettes taken from original essays. These essays are the extemporaneous writings of Chinese students at the Shanghai International Studies University. Some of the essays were recorded in the students' journals, others were written as parts of tests. In order to retain the originality of expression and to provide insights into the nuances of the Chinese language, we have chosen not to correct what many English teachers would call "grammatical errors." From the students' wording, the sensitive reader may draw a variety of inferences about Chinese thought.

It also is noteworthy that many of the Chinese students gave themselves English names in their essays. This is perhaps some evidence of the modernization of China.

CHAPTER ONE
PAST

Mr. Fang is an old teacher of a primary school where I studied for six years. His image, his rough voice, and his serious countenance linger in my mind and heart. His most prominent feature is his silence. Maybe his rough voice is not agreeable, and he does not want to talk too much. Maybe he believes that "Silence is gold." I learned much from him. He taught me to be upright, to be responsible, and to be diligent. He is a man to whom I show deep respect.

Mr. Fang is of medium height with dark and bushy eyebrows and deep-set eyes. His appearance probably gives you an impression that he is unapproachable. But that is quite misleading. As a matter of fact, he is very easygoing. He never blamed anybody in public. Even if you were late for twenty minutes, you were still permitted to enter the classroom. But he would stare at you in silence till you took out your textbook and were ready for the class. To most students his silence was the most severe blame. It was somewhat strange that nobody was late for his class after half a term.

Mr. Fang hates cheating. Once I did not prepare well for the exams, and I cheated in order to pass. Unfortunately, it was discovered by him. He frowned his dark and bushy eyebrows and glared at me with his deep-set eyes. Still he did not blame me in public. He just kept silence. This time I really felt ashamed of myself. Having that experience, whenever I want to cheat on an exam, I strongly feel his deep-set eyes glaring at me. Thus, I learned I should be responsible for what I have done.

(Written by "Henry," a Chinese student, then a senior majoring in English at Shanghai International Studies University, 1994.)

The Chinese word for teacher is *laoshi*, or "old master," a term signifying respect and deference. Since ancient times the teacher has been accorded high homage for the most part. But over the course of China's long history, the pendulum of respect has swung in both directions; and wars, rebellions, social movements, the coming of the West, and the Cultural Revolution all affected the status of the old master in various ways. However, the traditional view has remained much the same and is still current, as these quotations attest:

> "Under the sun, there is no other profession as sacred as that of the teacher."
> "Parents give one bones and flesh, the teacher gives one the soul."
> "One day's teacher, a life-time parent."
> "The teacher holds the golden key to knowledge."
> "The teacher is the engineer of the human soul."
> "The teacher is the link between the past and the future."

The Social Status of Teachers

For more than two thousand years the Chinese have worshipped Confucius (551-479 B.C.) as the father of Chinese education. In most Chinese schools, one finds a tablet inscribed with the characters, "Divine seat of the great accomplisher, supreme sage, foremost teacher, Confucius" (Yang, Lin, and Su 1989, p. 5). Mencius (372-289? B.C.), a close follower of Confucianism and a great educator himself, maintained that the teacher's position is comparable to that of a supreme ruler. According to Creel (1953), "Rulers wear a manner peculiar to their position, Mencius observes; but how much more should an air of distinction set apart the scholar who lives in the wide house of the world" (p. 68). Shun Zi (313-238? B.C.), a Confucian philosopher, exalted the teacher as follows:

> If a man is without a teacher or precepts, then if he is intelligent, he will inevitably be a robber; if he is brave, he will be a brigand; if he has ability, he will be a troublemak-

6

er; if he is a researcher, he will be interested only in strange phenomena; if he is a dialectician, his arguments will be absurd. But if he has a teacher and precepts, then if he is intelligent, he will quickly become learned; if he is brave, he will quickly become awe-inspiring; if he has ability, he will quickly accomplish whatever he undertakes to do; if he is a researcher, he will quickly push his investigations to their conclusions; if he is a dialectician, he will quickly solve every problem. Thus a teacher and precepts are the most important treasures a man can have; to be without a teacher and precepts is the greatest of misfortunes. The man who lacks a teacher and precepts exalts his original nature; he who has a teacher and precepts emphasizes self-cultivation. (Creel 1953, pp. 105-106)

Han Yu (768-824), a renowned writer and educator of the mid-Tang Dynasty, specified the roles of the teacher as "transmitting the way (principles or ideals) of life, instructing knowledge and skills, and solving puzzling problems" (Yang et al. 1989, p. 5). Han's contemporary, Liu Zhongyuan (773-819), another outstanding educator, celebrated his teacher. He believed that without his teacher's painstaking guidance, he could never have achieved his accomplishments (Liu 1979).

This tone of high respect was the rule for most of China's history until the late 1960s. Then, during the 10-year Cultural Revolution (1966-76), the rise of the bureaucratic elite prompted a decline of respect for educators. Universities and secondary schools were closed for some of the period; intellectuals were dismissed, killed, persecuted, or sent to labor in the countryside; the publication of scientific, artistic, literary, and cultural periodicals ceased; and the Red Guards attacked writers, artists, and educators. The ideology of political correctness destroyed the intellectual's status. But at the end of the Cultural Revolution, the former status of teachers was reasserted.

Deng Xiaoping, recognized as the architect of the current economic reform in China, repeatedly emphasized during his first several years in power that the key to the four modernizations is the modernization of science and technology. The task of training scientists and technicians rests with education and teachers. Deng further asserted that because China is a country with a huge population, once education was highly developed, then the strength based on China's human resources could not be matched by any other nation. The development of this highly effective education must rely on the development of teachers; therefore, teachers should be highly respected not only by their students but also by society (Deng 1983).

The re-establishment of teachers as honored persons was confirmed in 1985 when the National People's Congress passed a bill establishing September 10 as the date for an annual Teachers' Festival. On this day outstanding teachers at all levels of education are honored as model teachers.

Traditional Teacher Roles and Attitudes

Confucius believed that three factors promoted social progress: people, wealth, and education. When people multiplied and lived in wealth, education determined the pace and direction of social development. He explained that education positively influences people in their personal growth, contributing to the moral well-being of the whole society. In this process the teacher plays the crucial part (Sun 1993).

In Chinese history Confucius was the first to define how to be a teacher. His notions were further developed by his followers and became the basis for traditional teacher roles. This model continues to be followed by most Chinese educators. The model includes several components.

Teaching Without Discrimination. Recruiting students regardless of their family background and teaching without discrimination are Confucian principles for conducting a school. Anyone willing to learn and to demonstrate respect for the teacher should be enrolled. According to Confucius, a teacher's duty is to serve people of all walks of life and from all corners of the world by giving them good advice for self-cultivation and righteousness.

Teachers should neither refuse anyone nor retain those who wish to leave. Like good medical doctors who treat patients afflicted with various diseases, teachers are expected to educate students from diverse backgrounds and with various needs.

During his teaching career of 40 years, Confucius taught more than 3,000 disciples. The majority were of humble origins, such as Yan Hui, the son of a pauper; Zi Lu, a beggar; Chong Gong, the son of a homeless father; and Zi Gong, the son of a tradesman. Others, such as Sima Nu, bore noble family lineage. All were Confucius' favorite disciples, and most of them became government officials.

A simple, yet profound notion underlies this principle of Confucius: Most people are teachable, regardless of their backgrounds. Education is not solely for the privileged.

Moral Cultivation and Intellectual Development. Good teachers are not only knowledgeable but also morally cultivated. Education is a process of role modeling. In the Confucian tradition, the aim of education is to develop educated people who are qualified for public service, whose principal qualification is good moral character.

Confucian educational thought argues that moral cultivation goes hand-in-hand with intellectual development. Moral cultivation and the imparting of knowledge (a traditional act of teaching) share one process; they are fully complementary.

According to Sun (1993), the Confucian tradition holds that model teachers cultivate the moral character of their students in the following seven ways:

1. Cultivation of "Ren" or benevolence. The principle of Ren is to love people, to acknowledge others' rights, and to respect them as equals. Ren is practical. The practice of Ren starts with one's own family and extends to one's relatives and neighbors, broadening in range. Teachers project Ren to their students.

2. Goal-setting. Teachers should assist students in creating goals for their lives and striving to achieve these goals,

regardless of poverty or difficulties. Material temptations should not entice teachers or students.

3. Self-control and restraint. Dealing with oneself and others is critical to interpersonal and intrapersonal relations. Morally cultivated persons control their behavior and restrain their language, thereby complying with social standards. By observing the way a person treats himself and others, one can ascertain the attainment of moral cultivation.

4. Putting morality into action. Students not only listen to words, they also watch actions. As actions are the final manifestation of thought, teachers' deeds should match their wisdom.

5. Finding the golden mean. Actions do not always fit moral standards. Some may be lacking; others may exceed the ideals. Achieving a golden mean is essential.

6. Introspection. Contemplation and self-analysis augment understanding. Introspection leads to moral practices and self-correction.

7. Error correction. Mistakes and blunders are unavoidable. One should have the courage to recognize and correct errors, not to hide them. Practicing the former wins respect. But error detection and correction often require assistance. Therefore, teachers and students should welcome criticism and welcome opportunities to correct mistakes and to guard against repeating them.

Verbal instruction and teaching by personal example are two means of teaching. Verbal instruction augments understanding through explanation and reasoning; teaching by personal example models expected behavior and attitude. Of course, the two should match. According to Confucius, if teachers keep themselves righteous and set a good example in moral conduct, the students will follow that model spontaneously. Otherwise, in spite of their attempts to compel moral behavior, teachers will not inspire their students to follow the verbal instruction.

Hunger for Learning. One who dares to teach never ceases to learn. Persistence in learning is the prerequisite for being a teacher. According to Confucius, only when one takes such pleasure in learning that he forgets about his meal, his personal worries, and his age, can one pursue the lifelong career of a teacher.

Likewise, learning by rote cannot make one a teacher. Only those who gain new insights through reviewing the past are competent for the job. Teachers use knowledge of the past to look into and understand the present situation and to devise solutions to new problems. Acquired knowledge is the basis for the development of one's perception. Teachers have the two-fold responsibility of imparting that acquired knowledge to students and of exploring new knowledge.

Teaching benefits teachers as well as students. Instruction is not a one-way process. By helping students solve problems, teachers often gain insights. The educational process is a process of mutual development. Confucius said that among three travel companions, there must be at least one who can be the teacher. Knowledge can be learned but not exhausted. Complacency and self-satisfaction are destructive to the personal growth of a teacher.

Tireless Zeal and Optimism. By painstaking efforts in teaching and guiding students in learning, teachers manifest love for their students and devotion to their career. Good teachers possess tireless zeal for the profession, no matter how demanding their students may be. Confucius is a good model here. Teaching more than 40 years, he never refused a student. For example, Zi Lu, one of Confucius' 72 successful disciples, was considered unteachable because of "delayed thinking" and low moral standards. Confucius selected him as a disciple and through untiring efforts educated him to be an outstanding philosopher and statesman.

Similarly, teachers should demonstrate a positive and optimistic attitude toward their students, for the hope of the future lies in them. Because the younger surpass the older, Confucian tradition believes in the younger generation. In the long run, the student transcends the teacher. Just as parents see in their children the continuation of their lives, teachers observe in their students their moral and intellectual extension and growth. A student's failure or success becomes the teacher's failure or success.

Effective Teaching Methods. Perception is the basis of knowledge. Perception arises from social or physical interactions with society and the world. This is the epistemology of Confucian philosophy. One knows when one learns. One knows nothing more when one quits learning.

The two basic forms of learning in Confucian education theory are non-direct and direct. Non-direct learning includes book learning and classroom learning; direct learning occurs through personal interaction with subjects. Both forms are important. Through non-direct learning, students draw on the marrow of human knowledge accrued through generations. Direct learning employs hearing, observing, inquiring, and practicing, thereby accruing experience and maturation. However, such learning, unless coupled with critical thinking, keeps students on the surface of understanding. Learning with critical thinking immerses students in the essence of the issues. According to Confucian thought, this is the right way to learn.

But such learning and critical thinking are merely means. The end is practice, or putting the learning to work. Thus the complete role of teachers is to guide students in the cycle of learning, critical thinking, and practice.

Years before Socrates, Confucius introduced the methods of elicitation and induction. Confucian tradition maintains that learning should be based on the students' awareness, and teachers must promote initiative. Cramming is not desirable. Rather, elicitation and patient guidance are preferred.

Confucius believed that such an approach to education requires cooperation between teachers and students. Education is a true partnership. For students, a positive learning attitude is an important condition leading to success. Thus teachers should encourage learning as a passion and pleasure, questioning as a constructive way of learning, and honesty as the best policy in learning.

Modern, Post-Confucian Influences

Events of the recent past have both extended and modified Confucian education tradition. This recent past can be divided into three periods: the period before the reorganization of China into a republic, roughly 1800 to 1912; the period of the republic, 1912 to 1949; and the current era, which began with the communist revolution in 1949.

Prior to the Republic of China (1800-1912). Although Confucian education principles included recruiting students regardless of their family background and teaching without discrimination, formal education was a privilege of the rich for much of China's history. The difficulties of the Chinese language, which did not have an alphabet and whose written language was not the spoken one, made learning to read extremely challenging. Thus, historically, China had an extremely high rate of illiteracy. Even in the late 19th century, the nation's illiteracy rate was estimated to be more than 95% (Kuo 1915).

After China's defeat in the two Opium Wars (1842 and 1864), the Sino-Anglo-Franco War in 1858, the Sino-Franco War in 1885, the Sino-Japanese War in 1894-95, and the war waged by the League of Nations in 1899, the Chinese nation, led by the intellectual class, witnessed a painful retrospection. China's vulnerability resulted from a corrupt political system and historic negligence in the development of education and technology. Thus, working with the emperor, the intellectuals formulated three tasks that were designed to rebuild the nation and create a powerful, modern China: 1) political reform, 2) the introduction of Western technologies, and 3) the development of universal education.

In 1898, a memorable year in China's modern history, GuangXu, the young emperor, supported by Kang Youwei and Liang Qichao, well-known reformers, and their followers issued a series of decrees to initiate sweeping reforms in Chinese education. These reforms included the establishment of a system of modern schools to be accessible to most of the population, abolition of the "eight-legged essay" (so-named because of the exam's rigid and stilted eight sections) for the selection of government officials, and the introduction of short and practical essay examinations.

Through these efforts by the imperial power and the intellectuals, Chinese education underwent unprecedented rapid development. During the next ten years, the number of schools increased significantly. Table 1 shows this dramatic increase during the latter half of the decade, from 1905 to 1910. Similarly, the enrollment of students in all the types of schools grew from only 1,274 in 1903 to more than 1.6 million by 1910 (Kuo 1915, p. 108).

Table 1. Increase in Number of Types of Schools.

Year	Government	Public	Private	Totals
1905	2,770	393	224	3,387
1906	3,605	4,829	678	9.112
1907	5,224	12,310	2,296	19,830
1908	11,546	20,321	4,046	35,913
1909	12,888	25,688	4,512	43,088
1910	14,301	32,254	5,793	52,348

Note: Government schools were financed with government funds; public schools were financed with local public funds; and private schools were funded by private individuals and donations. Adapted from P.W. Kuo, *The Chinese System of Public Education* (New York: Steinman and Foltz, 1915), p. 108.

This rapid expansion of education called for an increase in the teaching force. However, for centuries, teaching had been regarded more as a form of art rather than as a branch of science. Therefore, schools for the professional training of teachers simply did not exist in China before 1897.

A number of Chinese educators of this period realized that teacher education was the key to the success of the nation's education "revolution." Prominent among them was Liang Qichao, considered by many as the preeminent modern education pioneer. Liang was the first to advocate the establishment of normal schools in China. According to Yang and colleagues (1989), Liang believed that teacher education was the foundation of all learning, and he warned that China could never change and promote intellectual learning unless the government first established normal schools.

Soon after, other influential Chinese reformers — Kang Youwei, Yan Fu, and Cai Yuanpei — joined Liang in promoting teacher education. Mass education was the way to save China, and establishing professional schools for the training of teachers was the key to promoting this great task.

In June 1896, the Qing Government advanced a proposal for establishing the Beijing Capital Normal University. The government document issued in this matter maintained that Western countries delegate high priority to teacher education, and their students learn effectively because teachers hold proper qualifications. The proposal advanced the idea that because China did not implement this practice, the nation's schools were ineffective (Sun 1993).

Notwithstanding this strong, Western-influence endorsement, the Beijing school was not the first to be established. In 1897, the first normal school in Chinese history was a forerunner institute, the Teachers Institute of Nanyang Academy, which was established in Shanghai. The institute included an affiliated elementary school, where students performed their practice teaching.

Then in the next year, in November 1898 after two years of preparation, the Capital Normal University formally opened in Beijing. This institution became the first government-run normal university. In 1902 the university admitted 79 students by examination, all of whom were residents of Beijing.

In order to give priority to the development of normal schools, the Ministry of Education formulated *The Outline for Educational Affairs* in 1903. This document stressed that schools must have teachers and that the government should expeditiously establish normal schools. Organizing junior normal schools for the training of elementary teachers was of the utmost importance. Finally, after nearly a decade, this document seemed to launch a nationwide flurry of development of teacher education institutions. Among the prominent institutions soon established during this period were:

15

- The Normal Institute Affiliated with Beijing Capital University, which was established four years after the founding of the Beijing Capital Normal University and later divided to become Capital University and Beijing Normal University;
- The Tongzhou Normal School (the predecessor of Nantong Normal School in Jiangsu Province), the first private normal school, which formally opened in April 1903;
- The Hunan Number One Normal School, founded in 1903 in Changsha, which later became Hunan Number One Provincial Normal School, where the communist revolutionary leader Mao Zedong earned his teaching qualifications after five years of study; and
- The Baoding Number Two Normal School, established in 1909, which in 1928 became Hebei Provincial Normal School.

In 1903, the Qing government also issued *Submitted Regulations on School Education*. In this document, the government classified normal schools into two categories: junior normal schools and senior normal schools. The former enrolled elementary school graduates to be trained as elementary teachers; the latter enrolled general secondary school and normal institute graduates to be trained as secondary school and junior normal institute teachers.

Junior normal schools offered two programs: the five-year full program and the one-year simplified program. The five-year program offered a 13-course curriculum, which included moral conduct, pedagogy, classics readings and lectures, Chinese literature, calligraphy, arithmetic, history, geography, chemistry, physics, biology, physical education, and drawing. Pedagogy consisted of five courses: principles of education, teaching methodology, classroom management, education systems, and internship-student teaching.

Optional courses varied from school to school and included agriculture, commerce, manual arts, music, and foreign languages. The average weekly study load ranged from 32 to 36 hours of classes. The students were provided with free tuition, room, and board on the condition that they would teach in an elementary school after graduation.

The one-year program prepared primary (grades 1-3) elementary school teachers. The curriculum was similar to that of the five-year program except that biology, calligraphy, and classic readings and lectures were not required.

The program for senior normal schools consisted of three components: 1) core curriculum, required courses for all students; 2) specialized courses, depending on the student's major; and 3) elective courses. The core curriculum, which was completed during the first year of study, included ethical morality, origin and evolution of classical philosophy, logic, Chinese literature, arithmetic, Japanese, English, and physical education. Specialized courses, which were studied during the second, third, and fourth years, consisted of four major areas: Chinese language and foreign language; mathematics, physics, and chemistry; history and geography; and botany, zoology, mineralogy, and physiology. All students were required to study pedagogy and psychology. Elective courses included an optional, additional year of study in aesthetics, experimental psychology, school health care, education systems, ethical morality, educational practice, or child study.

In addition to junior and senior normal schools, normal apprenticeship workshops and institutions to train vocational teachers were established to satisfy the urgent demand for teachers. After 10 months of study, normal apprenticeship workshop graduates were designated as associate elementary school teachers; after two years of education, vocational teacher graduates were placed as vocational school and apprenticeship workshop teachers.

The Republic of China (1912-1949). Puyi, the last emperor of China, was overthrown in 1911 as a result of the revolution led by the Cantonese Dr. Sun Yatsen. The Qing Dynasty ended, and the Republic of China was founded in 1912.

After the revolution and the founding of the Chinese Republic, teacher education underwent dramatic reforms. Normal schools of all types were upgraded to a higher level. Junior normal schools were renamed simply as normal schools, and schools that formerly fell in the jurisdiction of prefecture and county authorities were entrusted to the provincial governments. The senior normal schools became normal colleges.

In 1912 the new government promulgated two acts, the *Teacher Education Act* and the *Normal School Regulations*, which stipulated the role, objectives, programs, and curricula of teacher education institutions. As specified by the two acts, the objective of the normal schools was to train teachers for elementary schools, while normal colleges assumed the responsibility of teacher training for the secondary schools and normal schools. For the first time in China's education history, the two acts also recognized the rights of women in formal teacher training programs.

In 1913 the government introduced another major reform in teacher education — the establishment of a district system. Under this system the country was divided into six normal districts: Beijing District, regulating northern China; Shengyang District, managing northeastern China; Nanjing District, governing eastern China; Guangzhou District, overseeing southern China; Chengdu District, supervising western China; and Wuchang District, directing central China. Each district contained a normal college.

The years following the founding of the first teacher education institute witnessed rapid advancement in teacher training. By 1922, 275 normal schools enrolling 38,277 students (of whom 6,724 were women) had been established (Yang et al. 1989).

In 1922, a second structural reform in teacher education was decreed by the *Act on School System Reform*. Under this act, normal colleges again were renamed and reconstituted, either by upgrading them to universities or annexing them to existing comprehensive universities. For example, Beijing Normal College became Beijing National Normal University in February 1923. Chengdu Normal College merged with Chengdu University. The length of time required for teacher education was extended from five to six years. In addition, the curriculum was expanded from three to four component parts: core curriculum, major courses, minor courses, and elective courses.

Although the *Act on School System Reform* was designed to raise the standards of teacher education programs and to enhance the quality of the students, in practice the reform act weakened the development of teacher training. Therefore, in 1927, with the founding of the Nationalist Government in Nanjing, the teacher education system returned to the pre-1922 system. Five years later, the Fourth Nationalist Congress passed the *Bill on Educational Objectives and Educational System Reform.* This act specified that normal schools should be detached from general secondary schools and normal universities separated from comprehensive universities, that normal colleges or education departments of national universities should be annexed to normal universities, and that all teacher education programs should be public, with private teacher education institutes forbidden.

While much attention was given to teacher education during this period, the results of various reform attempts were decidedly mixed. National upheaval must be blamed to a degree. From 1921 to 1949, China experienced a succession of wars: the First Civil War, 1921-1927, in which the nationalists battled the warlords and then fought the communists; the Second Civil War, 1927-1937, in which the nationalists again battled the communists; the Anti-Japanese War, 1937-1945; and, finally, the Third Civil War, 1945-1949, which resulted in the retreat of the nationalists to Taiwan.

The People's Republic of China (1949-Present). After the communist victory in 1949, the government of the People's Republic of China formulated two special goals in education: to eliminate illiteracy and to provide universal education for all school-age children. To achieve these targets, the Communist Party and the government mobilized all possible personnel, many of whom were unqualified to teach. Government officials compelled authorities at all levels to design literacy classes and to establish elementary schools. In just a few years, literacy classes and elementary schools were proliferating even in remote villages and factories.

19

To ensure education for ordinary people, the government mandated three actions. First, language specialists devised a unified spoken language, Mandarin or Putonghua, and created the Pinyin system, a Romanized learning tool of the Chinese language that helped to make learning to read easier. Second, a national language committee simplified traditional Chinese written characters by reducing the number of strokes, thereby making it easier for students to memorize the characters. Third, the government promoted "conversationalization" of the Chinese written language so that common people could readily understand the written literature and, in turn, write what they desired to express. These initiatives assisted the drive toward universal literacy.

While the movement toward education for all was fairly successful in reaching much of the population, the quality of that education was questionable. The reformed, expanded education system demanded many teachers, and schools could not find enough competent faculty members. Consequently, over the next 40 years the Chinese government struggled to expand teacher education. Teacher education was restructured into three levels: district/county normal schools to train primary education teachers, municipal/regional junior normal colleges to train junior secondary school teachers, and provincial or national normal universities to train senior secondary school teachers and teachers of normal schools at the lower levels. The government also created incentive policies to boost the enrollment in normal schools and universities. One incentive was the universal stipend, by which normal school students nationwide received a uniform scholarship for their study and living expenses.

In 1949, when the communists first came to power, only 12 higher teacher education institutions were in operation, with a total enrollment of 12,000 students. In May 1950 the Ministry of Education issued the *Temporary Provisions of Beijing Normal University*, thereby establishing the legal foundation for developing higher teacher education. In August 1951 the central government called for the first national conference on teacher education. In July 1952 the government issued the *Regulations for Higher*

Teacher Education Institutions, which decreed that all schools and universities of education were independent institutions.

Responsibilities were redefined, structures and faculty reorganized, and resources re-allocated. To discuss problems and devise policies, in September 1953 the Ministry of Education convened the First National Conference on Higher Teacher Education. And by 1965, the number of higher teacher education institutions had been increased to 59, almost five times the number that existed in 1949, with an enrollment of 94,268 students (Department of Planning and Construction 1994).

With the incentives to eliminate illiteracy and to provide universal education for school-age children, the development of secondary normal schools (institutions preparing teachers for nursery schools, kindergartens, and primary schools) also increased. In 1949 the number totaled 610 with an enrollment of 152,000 students. By 1985 the number of schools had been increased to 1,028 with an enrollment of 558,000 students (Yang et al. 1989, p. 45).

However, the communist period has not been without problems. Teacher education, like education in general, was severely taxed during the ten-year Cultural Revolution. Student enrollment virtually ceased from 1966 to 1970. Existing curricula were labeled as bourgeois, revisionist, or counter-revolutionary. Progress in education was halted by political ideology that turned into political mayhem.

But at the conclusion of the Cultural Revolution in 1976, the central government reinstated most of the earlier education practices. In 1978 the socialist modernization drive and the socialist market economy reform ameliorated progress. From 1978 to 1987 the total number of institutions of higher teacher education again increased, this time from 157 to 260. The number of enrolled students increased from 249,940 to 507,963 (Department of Planning and Construction 1994).

In addition, to assist teachers affected by the setbacks of the Cultural Revolution, advancement schools at three levels (primary, junior secondary, and senior secondary) were instituted to provide inservice training programs.

These changes set in motion the reforms of Chinese education that have produced today's teacher education climate, which is the subject of the next chapter.

CHAPTER TWO
PRESENT

現在

While it may not be true that most American students attend school just for fun, academic achievement is less emphasized in America than in China. Figures:

1. The average weight of a Chinese student's schoolbag is 5 kilograms (approximately 11 pounds).

2. The average study hours of a student (include primary school and secondary school students) is 10 hours a day (not including additional lessons for worse students).

3. On Sunday, fifty percent of school children have to attend Sunday schools which help them with English, Maths and other subjects related to their studies.

Common believes held by school children:

1. Their lives are more "miserable" than adults, because even on Sunday, they have to study while most adults can relax and enjoy themselves.

2. They are forced to learn something which does not interest them at all, and forced out of touch with something they are interested in.

3. They live under too much pressure from both their teachers and parents who expect too much from them.

I really appreciate these words: "I can never be more than what I am." However, most Chinese parents think the opposite, for they "expect their sons to be a dragon and their daughters to be peonies" (from a Chinese saying). This may be one reason why academic achievements are emphasized. Other reasons are:

1. Social and historical influence. China is a country with long history, and throughout its long civilization, a basic belief is unchanged for thousands of years: that is, all occupations are base, only book-learning is exalted, that is to say, to be a schol-ar is on top of the society. In ancient times, government officials were chosen on the basis of "imperial examinations," which began in Sui Dynasty, the results of nearly 1300 years ago. Despite the fact that a lot of intellectuals were persecuted and despised dur-ing the "Cultural Revolution," the deep-rooted belief still has its influence on modern China.

2. Realistic emergency. The requirements for a better job are much more demanding. Any child who is not academically efficient will be in danger of joining the unemployment forces. In this way, many parents make it their responsibility to supervise their chil-dren's study because they think only in this way can their children have a bright future.

3. Educational system. One of my cousins, who is 14 years old now, once said to me, "We have small tests every Monday Wednes-day, and Saturday; big tests, every two weeks; and examinations every four months." We have key primary schools and key high schools which enroll academically excellent students every year. Those who are not very well in their studies have to attend techni-cal schools, special schools, and "common" high schools which are considered inferior. If you want to attend a famous university, you have to get very high results in the national examination for uni-versity applicants, otherwise your future is uncertain and gloomy.

(Written by "Stella," a Chinese student, then a senior majoring in English at Shanghai International Studies University, 1994.)

The People's Republic of China has the world's largest educa-tion system, with more than 1,100,000 schools of various types enrolling more than 330,000,000 students (Department of Plan-ning and Construction 1994). The government has initiated the principle of invigorating the nation by relying on science and education, making the best use of its limited financial resources to provide Chinese citizens with a steadily increased right to edu-cation. According to the Information Office of the State Council:

> By 1994 the country had altogether 683,000 primary
> schools with 128.2 million pupils, an increase of 4.7 per cent

over the 1990 figure; 82,000 regular middle schools with 49.817 million students, an 8.6 per cent increase over the 1990 figure; 1,080 universities and colleges with 2.799 million students, a 35.7 per cent increase over the 1990 figure; 1,172 schools of higher learning for adults with 2.352 million students, an increase of 41.1 per cent over the 1990 figure; 18,700 secondary vocational schools of various grades and types with 9.125 million students, a 39.8 per cent increase over the 1990 figure. (1995, p. 14)

Table 2 illustrates these changes in numbers of schools and students at various levels. The decline in the number of primary school students from 1980 to 1994 indicates the effects of China's "one-child family" population control policy, which was implemented in 1978.

Table 2. Comparative Educational Statistics 1965, 1980, 1994: Number of Schools and Student Enrollments.

Totals	1965	1980	1994
Primary schools	1,681,939	917,316	682,588
Student enrollment	116,209,000	146,270,000	128,226,220
Regular middle schools	13,990	87,077	82,358
Student enrollment	8,029,700	45,382,900	49,816,600
Universities/colleges	434	675	1,080
Student enrollment	117,129	1,165,304	2,798,600
Vocational schools	63,172	9,688	18,634
Student enrollment	5,081,800	2,397,500	9,124,900

Adapted from the Department of Planning and Construction, *Educational Statistics Yearbook of China, 1994* (Beijing: People's Education Press, 1994).

China's education system is divided into six categories:

1. Higher education (*gaodeng jiaoyu*) consists of institutions of higher education and research organizations.

2. Secondary education (*zhongdeng jiaoyu*) consists of the general secondary schools (three-year junior secondary schools and three-year senior secondary schools); junior middle schools,

which are part of nine-year compulsory education; specialized secondary schools, where teacher training schools and pre-primary teacher training schools are placed; vocational schools; skilled worker schools; and correctional work-study schools.

3. Primary education (*chudeng jiaoyu*) consists of five-year and six-year programs of elementary instruction.

4. Special education (*teshu jiaoyu*) is offered in separate schools at the primary level for six years and at the secondary level for three years.

5. Pre-primary education (*youer jiaoyu*) includes kindergartens and nursery schools.

6. Adult education (*chengren jiaoyu*) offers a wide range of education, including adult higher education institutions (radio/TV universities, workers' colleges, peasants' colleges, institutes for administration, educational colleges, independent correspondence colleges, evening schools, and short-cycle courses for cadres), adult specialized secondary schools (radio/TV, staff and workers' schools, cadres' schools, peasants' schools, correspondence schools, and inservice teacher training schools), adult general secondary schools (staff and workers' schools and peasants' schools), adult primary schools (workers' schools, peasants' schools, primary classes, and literacy classes), and adult technical training schools.

Compulsory Education

Promulgated as part of the general reform of Chinese education and specified as a national goal, the nine-year standard of compulsory education is becoming a reality. Compulsory education mandates six years of primary education and three years of junior secondary education. Dong states that compulsory education serves two purposes: "One is to enable the students to be ready for the employment and the other is to enable them to lay a solid foundation for entering schools of higher level" (1988, p. 5). According to the Information Office of the State Council:

> By the end of 1994 China had popularized five-year or six-year primary school education in areas inhabited by over

90 per cent of its population. The primary school per cent in 1994, an increase of 0.9 per cent over the 1990 figure, and 86.6 per cent of primary school graduates entered junior middle schools, an increase of 12 per cent over the 1990 figure. Nine-year compulsory education has basically been popularized in large and medium-sized cities and some economically developed regions. (1995, p. 14)

In order to develop compulsory education nationwide, the Chinese government is assisting economically deprived areas. In 1991 a "help-the-poor" education foundation was established, allocating 200 million yuan (approximately US$24.4 million) from state finances for education each year. Also, 30 million to 40 million yuan (US$3.7 to $4.9 million) in education fees paid by enterprises directly under the central government have been used exclusively for this purpose. The World Bank also contributed US$200 million.

To further augment state education appropriations, the government established the Hope Project. By the end of 1994 the government had collected more than 350 million yuan (US$42.7 million) in donations, established a back-to-school fund for children in disadvantaged areas who had discontinued schooling, and established 749 Hope Primary Schools. More than one million children who had been forced to leave school because their families were poor resumed their education (Information Office of the State Council 1995).

Primary Education. In order to adapt to the uneven development among different regions, primary education includes both five- and six-year programs. There are three types of schools: full-time elementary, rural elementary, and simple elementary. In full-time elementary schools the teaching program, principles, and materials are formulated and compiled by the State Education Commission. Each province, city, and autonomous region may make modifications in accordance with their own characteristics. Rural elementary schools teach only Chinese, arithmetic, general knowledge, and moral lessons. Simple elementary schools operate in various ways: part-time, alternate days, and mobile teaching, all emphasizing Chinese and arithmetic. Children begin school at age six or seven, with flexibility for sparsely populated minority areas.

The tasks of primary education are "to enable young children to develop morally, intellectually, physically, and aesthetically; to lay a foundation for the improvement of the national quality; and to cultivate the socialist citizens with ideals, morality, and discipline" (SEDC 1989, p. 2). The full-time teaching curriculum includes moral education, Chinese, mathematics, natural science, English, geography, history, physical education, music, fine arts, and physical labor. Moral education is based on the "five loves" — love of motherland, people, physical labor, science, and socialism — and focuses on patriotism, collectivism, politeness, and discipline. Physical labor necessitates using labor sites where children can perform tangible tasks.

Table 3 illustrates a typical first-grade schedule in a full-time primary school. This example is from Shanghai.

Table 3. Shanghai Full-time Primary School, Grade 1 Course Schedule.

Time	Monday	Tuesday	Wednesday	Thursday	Friday	Saturday
7:40 7:55	Teachers exercise in courtyard					
8:00 8:10	Homeroom					
8:15 9:00	Moral Ed	Chinese	Chinese	Chinese	PE	Chinese
9:00 9:45	Chinese	Physical Labor	PE	Math	Music	Math
9:45 10:15	Eye exercises and snack					
10:15 11:00	Chinese	Math	Math	Chinese	Math	Art
11:00 11:45	PE	Chinese	Music	PE	Chinese	Language self-study
11:45 1:10	Lunch (children go home)					
1:15 2:00	Music	PE	Writing	Nature	Hobby	Dismissed
2:15 3:00	Math	Math self-study	Chinese	Art	Dismissed	

Shanghai, one of the most progressive areas in China, has developed its own teaching materials, *Text for Nine-Year Compulsory Education, Edition for the Developed Area* (1993). The subjects of Chinese and mathematics dominate the elementary curriculum. During the first three years of primary education, basic literacy in Chinese is emphasized. As learning Chinese requires memorizing several hundred characters, reading, writing, listening, and speaking lessons are frequent. Students learn to read and write in pinyin, a method of writing the language using the Roman alphabet, and simultaneously transfer the knowledge to Chinese characters.

Three methods of calculation are used in the teaching of mathematics: oral (mental calculation), written calculation, and calculation with an abacus. Negative numbers, percentages, ratios, proportions, as well as some elementary statistics, also are taught.

English and sociology are introduced in grade 3; geography and biology are taught in upper elementary grades. Rounding out the curriculum are moral education, nature, physical education and health, music, fine arts, calligraphy, and physical labor. Self-study enhances specific study skills.

Prescribed Chinese texts reinforce Chinese values, moral precepts, and standards of conduct. For example, in "First Grade, First Semester Chinese" (*Text for Nine-Year Compulsory Education*, 1993), youngsters are taught Chinese by reading such passages as, "I like studying Chinese," "I am Chinese. I love my motherland," "The Five-Starred Red Flag is the national flag. We love the Five-Starred Red Flag," and "The earth is the mother of flowers. The sky is the mother of stars. Our motherland is our mother. We love our mothers. We love our motherland."

Many passages depict the values of collectivism, power distance, and intragroup harmony. "Collectivism is characterized by individuals subordinating their personal goals to the goals of some collectives" (Triandis, Brislin, and Hui 1988, p. 271). A key belief is that the smallest unit of survival is the collective. In Chinese society, the collective is the neighborhood and the *danwei*, or working unit. In Chinese schools, the collective is the class. Starting in the first grade and continuing into higher education, the class is an

31

intact group in which the teachers, not the students, move from classroom to classroom to teach their respective courses.

Power distance indicates the extent to which the people accept the fact that power in institutions and organizations is distributed unequally among individuals. Large power distance characterizes people who are comfortable with an unequal distribution of power, and they do not try to bring about a more nearly equal distribution. For example, prospective middle school students must take an entrance examination to gain admission into middle school. Only those students who score high are permitted to attend the outstanding key schools in the urban areas. Success in examinations is the key to a better education and to a better career.

Intragroup harmony means maintaining harmonious relationships with family members, friends, peers, and colleagues. As the class is the collective, students are conditioned to think in terms of service and the good of the people. Students tend to be well behaved, and they do learn.

But such political/societal didacticism is modified. Many reading passages for young children also focus on typical childhood characteristics, such as developing independence and self-reliance, as the following passage from "Do My Own Things By Myself" illustrates.

> Mother wants to help me wash my hands. I say, "No, I can do it by myself." Mother smiles. Father wants to help me organize my bag. I say, "No, I can do it by myself." Father smiles. (*Text for Nine-Year Compulsory Education*, p. 80)

Secondary Education. After graduating from primary school, students progress to secondary education. General secondary schools include a 3-year junior secondary school and a 3-year senior secondary school. Some systems have a 4-year junior/ 3-year senior plan; a few others have a 2-year senior school structure. Junior secondary schools advance the curriculum for the final three years of compulsory education. In addition, specialized secondary schools, vocational schools, skilled worker schools, and correctional work-study schools offer a variety of programs to meet the needs of the developing national economy.

According to the SEDC (1989), the academic year for junior secondary schools consists of two 20-week terms, 11 to 12 holiday weeks, and one or two weeks for flexible use. Six classes are offered each day, Monday through Friday. Classroom instruction involves 28 to 30 hours each week.

Required courses parallel those of primary education, with the addition of sociology for middle school, health education, physics, chemistry, vocational guidance, and computer. Elective courses include astronomy, fundamental medicine, formal logic, classical Chinese, and second foreign language. Many schools offer optional lectures — astronavigation, bioengineering, radioactivity — after classes to broaden students' education. Table 4 shows a typical distribution of classes at the junior secondary level.

Table 4. Junior Secondary School Curriculum.

Subject	Number of classes per week		
	Year 1	Year 2	Year 3
Political science	2	2	2
Chinese	6	6	6
Mathematics	6	6	6
English/foreign language	5	5	5
Physics		2	3
Chemistry			3
History	3	2	
Geography	3	2	
Biology		2	
Health education			2
Physical education	2	2	2
Music	1	1	1
Art	1	1	1
Total hours required courses per week	29	31	31
Elective courses	varies	varies	varies
Physical labor	2 weeks	2 weeks	2 weeks

Note. Adapted from State Education Commission of the People's Republic of China, *Education in China* (Beijing: State Education Commission, 1989).

Standards and Examinations

I took the 1985 National College Entrance Examination for students of arts. There were seven of them, namely Chinese, mathematics, politics, history, geography, oral English, and written English. I scored some 444, which was a little higher than the marks set for admission to universities in our Shanxi province. In our neighbor province, Henan, that year's marks were some 480, I heard. That is to say, different provinces have different marks for admission. And so do different universities and colleges, of course. 480 in our province meant a key university that year — two of my classmates went to key universities in Beijing that year. Both of them scored a little higher than 480. And the marks vary every year.

Maybe this kind of examinations are unfair for a lot of students, but certainly not for most of them. Up to now we have no better means to choose students to higher education effectively and economically. And what's more, we don't have enough enrollment figure due to lack of money.

(Written by "Frank," a Chinese graduate student at Shanghai International Studies University in 1994.)

As a number of researchers have noted, the Chinese culture traditionally has emphasized the importance of personal cultivation (Chen and Uttal 1988; Huang 1976; Stevenson 1992; Stevenson et al. 1990). Education is paramount because it is the means to self-cultivation. Chinese children are taught from an early age that good behavior, studying diligently, and a high level of educational achievement are important forms of self-improvement. They are taught that achievement is attained through effort and improving school performance is within one's control. Believing that teachers are more important than parents in influencing academic performance, Chinese parents set high standards of academic achievement for their children.

Likewise, examinations are a crucial feature of Chinese education. They determine whether an individual is eligible for more advanced training and what form that training will take. Beginning in the sixth year of primary school, students proceed to junior secondary school based on examination scores. Sixth-graders who score exceptionally well are admitted to the outstanding key junior secondary schools in the urban areas. Next, at the end of the third year of junior secondary school, students take examinations to determine placement in either key senior or regular senior secondary schools, specialized secondary schools, or senior vocational schools. Students who score poorly are placed in junior vocational schools and graduate as "workers."

One consequence of this system of values and standards is the pressure on students to succeed. According to Brauchli, "Parents put intense pressure on their children to study, sending even five-year-olds to boarding school and encouraging youngsters to do homework three hours a day" (1994, p. A1).

A national examination to determine higher education placement is administered each July and is taken by students in their third year of senior secondary school. For those earning distinguished scores, admission to the prestigious key universities is granted. Those whose score is higher than the admission cut-off may attend regular or adult institutions of higher education. The remainder may either retake the examination next year or join the labor force. The years of required training in these settings also vary according to the nature of the institution and its required courses. Brauchli (1994) found the following:

> Only 40% of primary-school graduates pass tests that let them into junior-high school; two-thirds finish. About one in eight Chinese reaches a general high school. Only three to four of every 100 Chinese pass the rigorous entrance exams for university. In the U.S. by contrast, nine out of 10 students do some secondary school, and three out of four go on to some kind of tertiary education. (p. A1)

Teacher Education

Eligibility to teach at the various levels is likewise determined by test scores. For example, future preschool teachers begin their teacher training at the end of junior secondary school. (The education level of Chinese preschool teachers is equivalent in years to that of a U.S. high school graduate.) The fact that they are enrolled in a secondary vocational school, rather than in a senior secondary school, indicates that they either did not score as well as their peers or chose to attend the institution. In contrast, future faculty for the higher levels of education commence their teacher training after graduation from specialized secondary schools.

Although their pay is low and there is little room for advancement, teachers generally are held in high esteem. Students rise when the teacher enters the classroom; the teacher greets the students by saying, "Tongxuemen, hao!" (Fellow students, how are you?). The students reply, "Laoshi, hao," which means, "Old master, how are you?" The greeting is typical and reinforces a classroom atmosphere of respect and friendship.

The teacher's overall mission is to nurture students who are moral, intelligent, and politically and socially conscious. Educators are expected to work hard in the profession, to take good care of the students, to be diligent, and to model appropriate behavior. Teacher education provides the means for teachers to reach these goals.

As in most countries, teacher education in the People's Republic of China can be categorized as preservice or inservice. Preservice teacher education prepares the student to enter the classroom, while inservice teacher education provides increased proficiency for those who already are teaching. Depending on the level at which the future teacher will work, their education is offered at the secondary and higher education levels. At the secondary level, teachers are trained for primary schools, kindergartens, and nursery schools; at the higher education level, secondary school teachers and higher education educators are trained.

Preservice Education. Four types of educational settings provide preservice teacher education: postgraduate schools of normal universities, normal universities and teachers colleges, professional teachers colleges, and teacher training schools. At the most prestigious level, two key normal universities train future faculty members for higher teacher education. These postgraduate schools of normal universities are located at Beijing Normal University and East China Normal University (Shanghai).

At the undergraduate level, normal universities and teachers colleges enroll senior secondary school graduates for a four-year training program for future senior secondary school teachers. The curriculum consists of five components: political theory (philosophy, history of Chinese revolution, and economics), foreign language, education courses (educational theories, psychology, and teaching methodology of Chinese language and literature), physical education, and basic specialized courses in major fields. Major fields are Chinese language and literature, history, mathematics, physics, chemistry, biology, geography, and physical education.

The program of study includes formal instruction in the required courses, student teaching, term examinations, laboratory work for those who are majoring in the sciences, and research training in which a graduation thesis is written during the senior year. Most institutions require students to reside on campus. Once enrolled, in addition to free tuition, students are provided with free room and board plus a stipend for other daily expenses. The amount of the stipend varies from province to province.

Professional teachers colleges enroll secondary school graduates for a two- or three-year training program as junior secondary school teachers. The curriculum includes political theory, foreign language, education courses, physical education, and specialized courses in a major field (Chinese language and literature, history, mathematics, physics, chemistry, or biology). The program of study is the same as that of the undergraduate level described above.

Teacher training schools enroll junior secondary school graduates for three or four years of additional schooling. Future teachers are prepared for primary schools, nursery schools, and kindergartens. The elementary school curriculum includes political science, Chinese language, mathematics, physics, chemistry, biology, hygiene, history, geography, foreign language, psychology, education theory, teaching methodology of elementary Chinese language, teaching methodology of elementary mathematics, teaching methodology of elementary science, physical education, music, and fine arts. Student teaching includes regular observation and participation and the final practice teaching. For final practice teaching, a total of eight weeks is required in the three-year program and 10 weeks in the four-year program.

The early childhood programs (kindergarten and nursery school) of teacher training schools enroll only female graduates of junior secondary schools. The curriculum and training are similar to the elementary school requirements.

Inservice Education. Inservice training programs offer four categories of training depending on the teacher's proficiency. First, remedial assistance programs are designed for teachers who are not competent or have not yet completed a formal teacher training program. The curriculum emphasizes mastery of teaching materials and methodology. Second, those who are generally competent in teaching but have not yet qualified in their formal preparation as teachers are required to take further study at the teachers advancement colleges or through radio or television programs and correspondence courses. Third, effective teachers and those who have the necessary educational preparation have opportunities to extend their knowledge, study education theories, consolidate their teaching experience, and pursue further individual studies. Finally, the outstanding teachers may advance in their mastery of both theories of teaching and subject matter in order to become experts and models in their teaching fields. Delivery systems are flexible and include options for part-time study, self-study, and short-term training.

Three levels of institutions provide inservice teacher education: provincial institutes of education or advancement colleges for senior secondary school teachers, regional and municipal institutes of education or advancement colleges for junior secondary school teachers, and county teachers advancement schools for primary, kindergarten, and nursery school teachers. Village or town supervisory centers also provide assistance for local primary school teachers. The county supervisory office and teachers advancement schools manage these centers.

Because inservice training is seen as an essential part of teacher education, all levels of formally approved inservice institutions are regarded as equal in standing to their preservice institutional counterparts. For example, provincial institutes of education are equal to normal universities; regional and municipal institutes parallel professional teachers colleges; and county teachers advancement schools correspond to normal schools.

In addition to the broad inservice training outlined here, all teachers participate, in general, in a half day of weekly inservice training. Inservice education also is provided by granting teachers sabbatical leave to pursue full-time study in professional and undergraduate programs. The professional, full-time program is a two-year course of study; the undergraduate program is a four-year program. For spare time and correspondence programs, the professional program is three years; the undergraduate program lasts five years. The curriculum is similar to that of the teachers colleges and normal universities, except that political science studies, physical education, foreign language, and student teaching generally are not required. The emphasis in these settings is on the major subjects the teachers teach and on education theory.

Funding Teacher Education

Funding for preservice teacher education institutions is obtained primarily through the national budget. Additional sources are provided by taxes and fees for education, enterprises, education revenues generated by work-study programs and services, and other state revenues. Table 5 shows the distribution of expenditures from these funding sources for 1992, as an example.

Total expenditures on education have risen steadily, from 50.4 billion yuan in 1989 to 54.9 billion yuan in 1990, 59.95 billion yuan in 1991, and 70.54 billion yuan in 1992 (SEDC 1993). Expenditures include both instructional expenses (including salaries and benefits, financial assistance for students, equipment, books and periodicals, operating expenses, support services, research, and administrative services) and capital investment for the construction of school buildings.

Table 5. Educational Expenditures for 1992.

Source	Amount in billions yuan
Total	70.54
1. National budget	56.49
2. Taxes and fees for education	6.16
3. Provided by enterprises	4.85
4. Education revenues from work-study programs and services	2.34
5. Other educational outlays financed by state revenues	0.70

Adapted from the Department of Planning and Construction, *Educational Statistics Yearbook of China, 1994* (Beijing: People's Education Press, 1994).

The specific funding sources for teacher training institutions depend on the level and type of institution. Funds for higher teacher education are provided in the state budget of higher education; teacher training schools are funded as part of general education. Financial support for most teachers colleges, normal universities, professional teachers colleges, and teacher training schools is controlled by the provinces, the autonomous regions, and the municipalities. Thus these types of institutions are funded locally as part of the local budget for higher education. Likewise, the funding for normal schools is part of the local budget for general education.

Normal universities, teachers colleges, and teacher training schools are funded according to the number of students enrolled and designated by the state plan. However, the standards for funding vary from the central government to local government, from provinces to municipalities, and from year to year. As a result of differences in economic strength among provinces and regions, the actual annual funding per student varies significantly. The more prosperous regions contribute more to education while the less prosperous provide less. Under special circumstances the state provides additional funds for teaching, research, and living expenses. The allotment depends on the financial capacity of the central and local governments and the status of the schools.

Funding for inservice teacher education programs is allocated by the local governments.

Keeping these variations in mind, a general picture of per-student annual expenditures for 1992 is shown in Table 6. A breakdown of instructional expenses and capital investments is shown for the regular institutions of higher education.

Table 6. Annual Expenditures Per Student in Local Budget 1992.

Schools by type and level	Amount in yuan
1. Regular institutions of higher education	
Instructional expenses	3874.98
Capital investments	727.47
2. Secondary teacher training schools	1757.08
3. Vocational schools	547.85
4. General secondary schools	311.79
5. Primary schools	141.65

Adapted from State Education Commission, The People's Republic of China, *Chinese Education at a Glance: Essential Statistics for 1992* (1993).

Problems and Issues

Chinese culture traditionally has emphasized the importance of education, but currently five issues are negatively affecting teacher education: shortages of teachers, inadequate teacher training standards, insufficient resources, low status, and questionable politics. Because of these issues, many younger Chinese students are not attracted to teaching as a career, even though education is highly valued.

Teacher Shortages and Inadequate Standards. Education is plagued by too few available teachers. First, colleges and normal universities are not matriculating enough graduates to teach in

41

secondary schools. In 1994, out of 1,080 colleges and universities enrolling a total of 2,798,600 students, only 241 institutions specialized in teacher education. Their enrollment was only 586,072 students (Department of Planning and Construction 1994). The demand for teachers majoring in Chinese, history, geography, biology, mathematics, physics, chemistry, physical education, English, fine arts, music, and political education far exceeds the supply of graduates.

Second, an overall shortage exists among primary and secondary school teachers, in particular junior secondary school teachers. Teachers colleges graduate an insufficient number of new teachers, many of whom have specialized in areas of study that do not reflect actual needs. And the majority of graduates are assigned to teach in senior secondary schools instead of junior secondary schools. In the primary schools, physical education, music, and fine arts teachers are lacking; and teachers of vocational subjects also are in short supply. Finally, the greatest obstacle to providing compulsory education is the extreme shortage of primary and secondary school teachers located in border and minority regions of China.

Present regulations require primary school teachers to graduate from normal schools, junior secondary teachers to graduate from professional teachers colleges, and senior secondary teachers to complete an undergraduate program. As a result of the Cultural Revolution, when diplomas were issued without the appropriate qualifications, a large number of teachers do not meet these standards. According to the Department of Planning and Construction of SEDC (1994), only 84.7% of the primary school teachers, 59.5% of the junior secondary teachers, and 51.1% of the senior secondary teachers are classified as "qualified" teachers.

Faculty development in institutions for teacher education is likewise inadequate. A scarcity of professors exists, while the number of instructors and assistants is sizable. The condition at this level is similar to the circumstances of the primary and secondary schools in that too few educators are available with training in certain subjects. Often faculty are assigned to areas with which they are unfamiliar, or certain subject areas can be taught by only one individual. Thus opportunities for collegial collaboration and consultation are rare in some fields.

Resources and Status Problems. Although teaching responsibilities increase every year, resources do not. Salaries, financial support, up-to-date equipment, and technology are lacking; library holdings are small and often unavailable for circulation; new school construction often has been delayed for years; and many buildings are outmoded and in need of repair. In addition, unpaid back salaries in some cases have adversely affected the stability of the teaching force.

Once an attractive career, teaching has fallen in social status. Coupled with low pay, low status is making it more difficult to attract new teachers. The highly structured examination and employment systems also have adversely affected education. In 1986, only 31 (36%) of the 86 education graduates in the Nanyang Region of Henan Province actually registered for a teaching position (Yang et al. 1989, pp. 89-90). According to Po:

> Hunan province lost 6,292 primary and secondary school teachers from 1990 to 1992 — 2% of the total teaching force. Of the 5,138 who changed professions, 96.8% were forty-five years of age or older, and the vast majority of them held positions in high school, junior high, or the upper elementary grades. They were the cream of Hunan's rural teaching core. (1993, p. 63)

Many believe these statistics are likely to get worse because of China's open-door employment policies and the desire of many younger students to make money in the burgeoning socialist market economy.

Questionable Politics. Two questionable political trends in teacher education warrant attention: the "name only" raising of institutional status and the improper imitation of comprehensive universities among the institutions of higher teacher education.

43

Some normal schools have inappropriately changed their names to professional teachers colleges, and some teachers colleges have unscrupulously changed their names to normal universities. These name changes without changes in curriculum design undermine genuine efforts to improve the quality of teacher education.

In somewhat similar fashion, some teachers colleges and normal universities imitate comprehensive universities by changing their programs at the expense of preparing secondary teachers. The parallel curriculum design neglects specialized education programs and courses, discourages education research, and downplays teaching practice. Finally, some colleges concentrate chiefly on the number of college diplomas at the expense of program goals and student outcomes.

An indication of these problems is evident in the following excerpt from a letter received from a Chinese associate professor, who was applying to a doctoral program at an American university in 1995:

> The winter vacation is over and I am fully engaged at present: enrolling new students, working out the teaching assignments. The program hasn't got any assignment this semester, so its teachers will all work for the American program and I'll have to see to 20 classes, together with 22 Chinese teachers and 5 American teachers. I have to teach 20 periods myself. Moreover, I have to continue with the editing of a collection of essays on the contrastive study of Chinese and English languages and cultures (which took me the whole winter vacation, including the traditional Spring Festival) and do some more reading since I have been invited by another university to be on the committee when a M.A. candidate defends her thesis. Besides I have been involved in an English-Chinese dictionary compiling work, which I find too time-consuming. Of course you can also imagine the amount of housework I have to see to: cooking, cleaning, washing, etc. I feel that there is so much to learn and to do but I have so limited time and energy as well as ability, but I always try hard to do my best. As a matter of fact, I am doing what is meant for 2-3 people here.

The college where this professor taught recently was upgraded to a comprehensive university. Now the university enrolls more students and issues more diplomas in a wider variety of programs, but the faculty remains the same size. Consequently, the faculty are overworked, and the quality of the programs and its graduates is questionable.

CHAPTER THREE
FUTURE

The open-door policy has brought in vitality to China almost in every sector. Undoubtedly, the education system is also subject to reform. It should be admitted that the tuition-charging measures in some leading universities are a creative and significant step of the educational reform. This new reform will result not only in the alleviation of the educational fund shortage, but also in the enhancement of education policy. Therefore, it is a feasible method and will be followed by many other universities. This will, I believe, lead to an educational revolution in China.

As we know, educational funds in universities are allocated by the state, which is considered a heavy burden to the fiscal budget. Yet the funds are so limited that teaching equipment remains inadequate and teachers be poorly paid. Under such circumstances, China's education is seriously hampered and restrained. This, no doubt, will lead to the degradation of the education quality. Therefore, this is the high time for change. Some Chinese leading universities including Beijing University, Shanghai International Studies University, and Shanghai University of Finance have thought of new ways to solve the problem. High school students now are required to pay tuition upon their entrance into these universities. Thus the money raised through tuition can be used to improve the educational environment. This is beneficial to the universities as well as to the students themselves. But there still exists a common fear that students from poor families might shun away from it. In fact, such fear is unnecessary. Along side with the tuition charging system, the universities have put forward measures to aid those poor students. For example, no-interest loans are accessible for the economically crippled students. They can pay back the loans when they earn money after gradu-

ation. A universal scholarship is also available for them if they behave excellently. Another beneficial effect is that the tuition-charging system will push every student to work hard instead of idling time, which will enhance ultimately the education quality.

Therefore, the new measures are feasible in China. This can be seen in the cases of newcomers in these universities. This will push China's university education to a new stage.

(Written by "Dupont," a Chinese student, then a senior majoring in English at Shanghai International Studies University, 1994.)

Recently several Chinese leading universities including SISU were approved by the State Education Commission to accept high school graduates who pay their tuition. It is said that more and more universities will follow suit. But I cannot see the light of this reform, which, in my opinion, will inevitably lead to "noble schools" because those "beggar-born deserts" would be denied of the chance of attending universities.

Some people say that students who study at their own expenses will treasure their lives on campus instead of idling away their time for they are paying to study. However, if money can ensure their entrances to university, will those rich students in high school "treasure their lives on campus instead of idling away their time?" Chances are that those students from rich family tend to be more gaudy and idle, as we have seen in our university. For example, in a class nearly half of the students who pay their tuitions failed in the mid-term exam last year. Anyway, if one studies just for money's sake, what can we expect of him?

Others say that all the universities will have a variety of financial-aid programs to help those talented but economically-crippled students. But I am afraid that they would have no chance to enjoy those programs because their families will be frightened by the high tuition and thus will persuade them to turn to other universities which are temporarily free.

In our much-changed society, money is becoming more and more important and it seems to me that nowadays everything is a bargain across counter. I hope that our education system will not be a bargain.

(Written by "David," a Chinese student, then a senior majoring in English at Shanghai International Studies University, 1994.)

Sweeping education reforms have been proposed, including reform in higher education and specifically in teacher education. As the open-door policy and the socialist modernization drive enter new stages, efforts to establish a socialist market economy, accelerate the pace of reform, liberate and develop productive forces, improve overall economic performance, and enhance national strength are intensifying. Education is directly affected, and thus new tasks and requirements have been set. Much of this chapter will strike readers as idealized. Indeed, any vision of the future must be so. Whether the visions and goals can be realized remains to be discovered.

In February 1993 the Central Committee of the Communist Party, together with the State Council, officially distributed the *Outline for Reform and Development of Education in China*. This document details strategic tasks to guide education reform in the 1990s and into the next century. According to the *Outline*, "We must make education a strategic priority as it is of fundamental importance to China's modernization drive to raise the ideological and ethical standards of the entire population as well as its scientific and educational levels" (p. 1).

The main tasks include: 1) implementing state education policies; 2) gearing education to the needs of the modernization drive, the world, and the future; 3) augmenting education reform and development; 4) improving the quality of the workforce; 5) training large numbers of capable people; and 6) establishing an education system suited to a socialist market economy, thus restructuring politics, science, and technology.

Since the founding of the People's Republic of China in 1949, marked progress has been made in education. A socialist education system has been established, qualified personnel have been trained, and school conditions have improved. Education reform has progressed steadily: the nine-year compulsory education program has been implemented, primary education is becoming universal, and technical and vocational education has developed. Today more than 50% of the students in senior secondary schools are registering for or are studying at secondary technical and vocational schools. Higher education also has developed briskly. Enrollments have increased, and a comprehensive system featuring a variety of disciplines is in place. Education for adults and minorities has been founded, and international exchange opportunities are available.

However, much remains to be done. Overall, education is insufficiently developed, and the strategic importance of education has not been fully recognized in the area of practical endeavors. Investment in education also is inadequate. Teachers' salaries and benefits remain low, and working conditions often are marginal. Educational philosophy, teaching concepts, and methodologies are divorced from reality to varying degrees; ideological and political work at schools needs to be strengthened; and the education system and its management mechanisms cannot meet the needs of the continual restructuring of the economy, politics, science, and technology. As the economy expands and the reform deepens, serious efforts must be made to solve these education problems.

The Central Committee and the State Council proposed eight principles for establishing a socialist education system suited to the current and future needs of China:

1. As the basis of the modernization drive, education must be given the strategic position at the top of the list of development priorities.

2. The Party must continue to exercise leadership over education, and education must adhere to a socialist orientation so as to train builders of the country and successors to the socialist cause who are developed morally, intellectually, and physically.

3. So as to promote all-around social progress, education must serve the socialist modernization drive, be integrated

52

with productive labor, and be geared to the needs of the central task of economic development.

4. We must adhere to the policy of reform with a view to improving the educational system, structure, teaching concepts, and methodologies. We must boldly assimilate the advances of other cultures, courageously blazing new trails and experimenting with ways to improve our socialist educational system.

5. We must follow the Party's and State educational policies, observing the laws governing education and improving the quality of instruction and the efficiency of schools.

6. We must rely on teachers; constantly work to raise their political and professional levels; and improve their working, studying, and living conditions.

7. Efforts must be made to encourage governments at all levels and the general population to contribute to the development of education, though education should continue to be financed chiefly by government allocation supplemented by funds generated through various other sources.

8. We must proceed from the specific conditions of China and in accordance with the necessity for both unanimity and diversity to carry out a diversified approach to education, train a variety of qualified personnel, and follow a course in education suitable for China as a whole as well as for its different regions. (1993, p. 2)

The Chinese endeavor aims at significantly improving the education level of the population by the end of this century. That endeavor includes goals to enhance pre-employment and job-related training after employment for both the urban and rural workforce, to increase the number of capable personnel in all fields to meet the needs of the modernization drive, and to construct a socialist education system suited to China's specific conditions. The ultimate goal is to improve the quality of the entire nation by training as many qualified personnel as possible. Schools of all categories and levels will conscientiously implement a policy of education that will serve the socialist modernization drive, will be integrated with productive labor, and will train builders of the country and successors to the socialist cause who are morally, intellectually, and physically well-developed so that the overall quality of education reaches a new level.

Four education objectives have been proposed for the 1990s. First, China will make nine-year compulsory education universal, including technical and vocational education at the junior secondary level. Second, enrollment in technical and vocational schools at the senior secondary level will be increased, thus providing education to graduates from junior and senior secondary schools who are unable to continue their study at other institutions of higher learning. Third, some 100 key colleges and universities will be founded to offer specialties that parallel advanced, international universities in terms of quality coursework and research. Finally, illiteracy will be reduced to less than 5%, as job-related training and continuing education programs will be developed.

In order to accomplish these objectives, China must escalate education reform efforts, maintain coordinated development, increase investment in education, improve the professional competence of teachers, enhance the quality of education, stress efficiency in education, prepare regional plans, and encourage all sectors of society to participate in the development of education. By the year 2025, the Chinese envisage a more mature and refined socialist education system and the realization of the modernization drive.

The Action Agenda

Basic Education. As basic education is fundamental to the Chinese, the Compulsory Education Law, or nine-year compulsory education (NYCE), will be rigorously implemented. To ensure that governments, communities, and parents require school-age children to attend school, the government will institute evaluation, monitoring, and award/punishment systems. If an organization or individual employs school-age children when the children should be in school, they will be punished accordingly.

To develop basic education, school conditions will be improved and gradually standardized. Primary and secondary schools will shift their emphasis from training a limited number of learners to improving the quality of the nation as a whole. Schools will be reorganized to meet the needs of all students, working to improve students' ideological and moral integrities, scientific and educational levels, professional skills, and physical and psychological conditions.

Technical and Vocational Education. Technical and vocational education (TVE) is viewed as an important pillar of industrialization, large-scale production, and modernization. Government departments, business enterprises, and public institutions now are required to promote its development and to become actively involved so that TVE schools of various disciplines and levels will flourish.

TVE currently is offered at secondary specialized schools, skilled-workers schools, vocational high schools, university-level schools, and short-term technical training institutes. By the end of the century, all trades in key cities and in every county will establish one or two training centers for demonstration purposes. Also, a large number of short-term training courses will be developed, thus forming a TVE network.

The development of TVE will be based on local economic development needs. In areas with nine-year compulsory education in place, the development of post-junior secondary TVE will be stressed. In areas where compulsory education is lacking, TVE will be offered to primary school graduates who are unable to study at a junior secondary school. Post-senior secondary TVE programs will be available to graduates who are unable to enroll in colleges. TVE courses also will be provided in some regular secondary schools.

The differing TVE schools will meet the needs of local development and of the socialist market economy. Joint sponsorship for education development, under the guidance of the government, will be encouraged. Productive labor will be integrated with teaching. Loans will be available to develop school-run enterprises that will enable schools to develop independently.

Gradually the schools will be supported by revenues generated by local factories or farms, rather than through government subsidy.

The principle of "training before employment" will be followed. People who have received technical and vocational education will have a priority in employment. Jobs requiring special skills will be open only to those with a job-qualification certificate. Before they can be hired, people without prior training will be required to obtain job-related training.

Higher Education. Higher education includes short-cycle, undergraduate, graduate, and other higher degree education opportunities designed to train high-level, specialized personnel. In the 1990s higher education will be geared to the needs of accelerating the reform and promoting the modernization drive. New approaches will be explored to make the system more diversified, thereby improving its quality and efficiency.

Internal efforts will drive higher education development. Goals and priorities will be devised to take into account differences among areas, disciplines, and schools. Standards for categorizing institutions will be set and corresponding policies formulated to make the division of labor among the institutions more rational, with each playing its unique role. Major efforts will be made to develop local special education and to meet the needs of rural areas, township enterprises, and service industries. Efforts will be made to train more postgraduate students, and new specialties will be developed in the applied disciplines. Two-tier management at government and provincial levels gradually will be introduced; and the power of provinces, autonomous regions, and municipalities to make education decisions gradually will be enlarged.

Funds from central and local governments and private individuals will finance the development of approximately 100 key universities that will offer specialized disciplines. By the year 2000, officials speculate that these select universities will rank among the most advanced in the world in terms of teaching quality, scientific research, and management.

Scientific and technical research will conform to state policies and adhere to the concept that science and technology constitute a primary productive force. Research efforts will encourage technology development, wider application of technology, and the establishment of technology information services. An expert team will be convened to undertake major national projects and to develop new technologies. Plans will be designed to build key national laboratories and engineering research centers that will match those of technologically advanced countries.

Teaching and research in philosophy and the social sciences will be linked to reality and guided by the theories of Marxism. Emphasis will be given to the need to study and solve theoretical and practical problems so as to develop knowledge and espouse socialism with Chinese characteristics.

Adult Education. Adult education, a new system for the Chinese that will expand traditional school education into lifelong education, will play an important role in promoting economic and social development. The curriculum is planned to meet the needs of employees. Study and practice will be integrated: Attention will focus on job-related training, continuing education, and major programs to update the knowledge base of employees. The government also will establish a certificate system, qualification examination, and testing system.

Major efforts will be made to develop rural adult education, to create general and technical schools, and to enhance the literacy levels of rural workers. The goal will be the elimination of illiteracy in the 15- to 40-year-old age group. This will be accomplished by setting strict standards and merging general education with TVE. Also, governments at all levels will allocate more funds for literacy programs.

Collaboration will occur between regular schools and adult academic equivalence education. Schools that offer adult education but are ineligible to grant official diplomas will award a certificate to their graduates. Students desiring to obtain a state-recognized diploma will take either a qualifying national examination or a self-study examination. Self-study examinations will be designed to reward individuals who teach themselves in their spare time.

Minority Education. China is a country of many nationalities, although 94% of the population are Han nationality. Minority nationalities include Mongolians, Tibetans, Uighurs, Koreans, Manchus, and 50 others. The Chinese Constitution stipulates that the various nationalities have the freedom to use and further develop their unique spoken and written languages.

Preferential education policies will be formulated for the poverty-stricken, minority-nationality areas. Allocation of funds by both central and local governments will be increased. Local governments will provide incentives for graduates from universities and colleges who volunteer to work in border areas or minority-nationality regions. Programs to support education development in these regions will be managed by economically stable provinces and cities. The minority-nationality regions will design education goals and objectives to meet their specific needs.

Special Education. More attention and support are promised for education for the physically challenged. All levels of government will consider such special education to be a component of the total education system. Accommodations will be provided either independently in special schools or in regular schools. Funding will be increased, and all sectors of society will be encouraged to contribute to the education of the physically challenged.

Long-Distance Learning. Radio and television are proposed as means to augment the use of modern teaching techniques. Efforts will be made to construct receiving stations and broadcast networks for satellite education programs. By the end of the century, the Chinese authorities envision a national audiovisual teaching network serving most townships and remote areas.

International Exchange and Cooperation. Drawing on the successful practices of other countries in the development and management of education, the Chinese authorities will intensify international exchange and cooperation. In accordance with the policy of permitting people to study abroad, encouraging them to return, and allowing them to come and go freely, the Chinese government plans to send more students overseas, considering them valuable assets of the nation.

State policies regarding overseas study will be strictly enforced. Officials will support study and research abroad by encouraging the students to return on completion of their study in order to participate in the socialist modernization drive. The enrollment and administration of foreign students in Chinese universities also will be reformed, and exchange and cooperation between Chinese universities and foreign institutions will be strengthened through joint training and joint research programs. Additional efforts include offering more Chinese-language classes for foreigners and participating in more international conferences.

Moral Education. The major tasks of moral education are 1) applying Marxism-Leninism, Mao Zedong thought, and the theory of building socialism with Chinese characteristics to educate students and 2) following a firm political orientation to train a new generation of builders of socialism who have lofty ideals, moral integrity, a sound education, and a strong sense of discipline. Chinese authorities propose to intensify moral education through the organization of roles and conduct in primary and secondary classrooms, the curriculum content in which texts abound with descriptions of exemplary figures, and extracurricular activities that promote patriotism and community spirit, particularly those related to the organization of the Young Pioneers.

The Young Pioneers is a primary-school organization in which students act as role models for their peers. Organized at three levels — one brigade, two or more companies, and two or more small squads — membership is open to children between their seventh and fifteenth birthdays. Membership is attained through invitation by the steering committee of the company, which reviews applicants on the basis of their willingness to serve the people and to promote the functions of the organization. Triangular red scarves readily identify members of the organization. Using Marxist theory, viewpoints, and methods, students approach practical problems, increase their solidarity with work-

59

ers and peasants, and learn to engage in practice as they mature. Students are trained to view the world scientifically, to serve the people by "enhancing their ability to resist decadent ideas of the exploiting classes, in particular bourgeois liberalization," and to maintain a firm faith in the theory of building socialism with Chinese characteristics (Hawkins and Stites 1991).

Reform efforts include paying more attention to educating students in China's cultural traditions. Primary and secondary students will be taught to behave in a civilized manner. In light of actual conditions in schools of differing categories and levels, a scope and sequence in ethics will be determined and teaching materials and methodologies on moral education will be enriched.

The teaching of ethics will be the responsibility of all teachers. Not only will ethics be an integral part of the curriculum, but also teachers will model appropriate behavior. An expert, full-time team of teachers will be trained in political and ideological education in institutions of higher learning, and their work will be supplemented by that of part-time teachers. Teachers responsible for the courses on moral education, class supervisors, and cadres of the Youth League and Young Pioneers will play important roles in primary and secondary schools. Training will be offered to people so that they can increase their ideological and political integrity, enhance their understanding of state policies, and improve their professional competence. The material benefits of these ranks also will be increased.

Specific Reforms

Establishing a socialist market economy is the foremost reform objective of the Fourteenth National Party Congress. In the 1990s, along with economic, political, scientific, and technological restructuring, comprehensive education restructuring will be administered in an ordered way. The restructuring pace will be accelerated and the system reformed to make it less restrictive. Education restructuring promises to improve teaching quality, raise the level of scientific research, enhance efficiency, and, of course, make education better serve the socialist modernization drive.

The government plans to expedite efforts to draft revised basic laws and regulations governing education so that by the end of the century a legal framework for education will be in place. Following are highlights of the proposed reforms:

Reform in Education Funding. Currently education funding is provided chiefly by the central government. In the future, funds for education also will be allocated from other sectors. Local governments will finance basic education; the central, provincial, autonomous, and municipal governments will fund higher education; trades, enterprises, and public institutions will finance TVE and AED. In addition, citizens will contribute to education funding through taxes, tuition fees, and educational funds.

Because higher education is not compulsory, universities will institute a tuition system, rather than provide the historically free education for those who are qualified academically. Students will be charged for tuition, living expenses, and miscellaneous fees. University loan plans will be established to assist students from financially disadvantaged families. The state, business enterprises, and public institutions also will establish scholarship programs for outstanding students, both academically and morally.

As a pilot program, Shanghai International Studies University initiated the tuition charge system in 1993. Chinese students have viewed this reform measure with mixed feelings. Following are two examples:

> This reform can stimulate students to study hard and make full use of their time. Many students in the universities which are free are idling away every day, except for the period of examination. Too many of them pass through the years without recognizing that time is their most valuable gift. They have so much of it and can't increase it substantially. But if they must study at their own expense, they will consider how to take advantage of these four years. Every sec-

ond counts and every chance will be firmly grasped. Especially, every material will be in full use — reading room, library, radio and television. Maybe some students from financially restrained families can't afford such a tuition. But in my opinion, they can overcome this problem by supporting themselves through part-time job. I have been a governess for three years during the study in this university. My income would be enough to pay the tuition if there is one. And students can get working experience from their part-time jobs and make preparation for their future jobs. They should support themselves to get independence and cultivate their personal ability. On the other hand, all the universities will have a variety of financial-aid programs to help those talented but economically-crippled students to finish their education so there is no possibility that universities would become "noble schools."

(Written by "Eddy," a female student, then a senior majoring in English at Shanghai International Studies University, 1994.)

As we all know that, China is still a developing country and the living level of ordinary people is not high. The average income of ordinary families is far from the amount of the tuition which is announced by some leading universities. Therefore, the high tuition is really a heavy burden for most families. Some students, in order to solve the family economic problem, have to give up their former wishes and turn to other universities which are temporarily free. It is worth noting that these universities are also subject to the economic change. Some students, although talented, will be denied the chance of attending the leading colleges if they are from financially-restrained families. But these universities do not worry about the number of applicants since there is a rich-class in China. In spite of reform policy, there are still a lot of students applying for these universities. Among them, there are some good students, but others are not as good as supposed. Depending on the richness of their parents, they only want to have a chance to enter the university not for studying but for their vanity. They only focus on their future certificates rather than the knowledge available. Although they are overshadowed by those diligent students in the high school, yet they have the opportunity to study in a key university, which is a honorable thing in other people's view. When they come into the university, they bring the bad atmosphere to the campus. There are more and more affairs of violation against the university rules or even national laws. This phenomenon also influences other students' mood and studying. The whole quality of the university students has been reducing. Undoubtedly it will affect the reputation of the universities.

We have realized how important the role education plays in a country's development. In the past, universities present the greatest opportunities for those excellent students in order to encourage their further studies but at present, they care about rich students. It is a pity that good students have to give up the leading universities; it is a greater pity that the key universities have given up those excellent students. I am ashamed at this tragedy which is caused by money-oriented thought. A university is a palace of knowledge not an industrial enterprise.

(Written by "Lin," a female student, then a senior majoring in English at Shanghai International Studies University, 1994.)

Reform in Educational Leadership. Under the guidance of the central government, local governments will be responsible for making plans and for administrating education at the secondary level and below. The state will decide the length of schooling, the curriculum and its criteria, teacher recruitment policies, qualifications for teachers, staff considerations, and teacher and staff salaries. Governments at the provincial, autonomous regional, and municipal levels will decide on the specific length of schooling, scale of yearly enrollment, teaching plans, selection and approval of textbooks prepared at the provincial level, and the maximum number of teachers and their salaries.

Governments at the county and township levels will incorporate education into their overall plans for economic and social development and adopt a level-by-level approach for administering basic education, technical and vocational education, and adult education. Vigorous measures will be taken to manage and promote comprehensive reform of urban education.

A headmaster responsibility system will be devised, in which a principal manages each school. One of the principal's responsibilities will be to establish partnerships between the school and local enterprises, public institutions, and neighborhood committees. Partnership programs will encourage financial support, participation, and collaboration from diverse sectors in an attempt to link schools with the real world.

Reform in Higher Education. The goal is to establish a higher education system in which universities independently provide education geared to the needs of society under the leadership of the government. Restructuring will be aimed at defining the relationships between government and colleges, between central government and local government, and between the State Education Commission and various ministries and commissions.

The principle of separating government from institutions of higher learning will guide the government and college connection. Laws will be drafted specifying the rights and duties of higher learning institutions, so as to make them legal, independent bodies. Institutions will be given greater freedom in enrolling students, changing the number of specialties, adjusting organizational structure, promoting and demoting cadres, allocating funds, granting professional titles, paying salaries, and dealing with daily circumstances. The institutions will acknowledge their rights and devise a self-governing mechanism that will operate independently to meet the needs of economic and social development.

Currently, the state controls the total number of enrollments at universities. This design guarantees the supply of qualified personnel to meet the needs of major state construction projects, state defense construction, culture and education, basic sciences, and remote areas with harsh working conditions. As the number of students on contract with employers and the number of self-supported students increases, the state will provide only macro-control in terms of enrollment guidance, while each university will determine its enrollment targets and limits based on the actual capacity of that university.

Instead of exercising direct administration over institutions of higher education, the government will macro-control and adjust through legislation, funding, planning, information service, policy guidance, and secondary administration. Advisory, evaluation, and assessment bodies comprising various experts, including educators, will recommend principles, policies, and strategic plans for higher education. Theoretical research will be initiated in education reform and development, with a focus on decision making and practical application.

The central government will continue to exercise direct administration over key universities that play a leading role in higher education, as well as over several special universities that are too difficult for local governments to administer. Under the guidance of central government policies, the responsibilities and rights of administration over local universities will be delegated to the provincial, autonomous regional, and municipal governments. They will make decisions regarding enrollment quotas and course offerings and will be responsible for raising revenues and preparing a comprehensive plan for job assignments of graduates.

The State Education Commission will be responsible for making overall plans, guiding policy development, coordinating management efforts, monitoring, and providing essential services to the respective sectors. Other ministries and commissions will focus on personnel needs, assist the State Education Commission in the training of personnel, and exercise administration over the universities under their jurisdiction. Under state macro-guidance, ministries also will manage enrollment of their own universities, determine specialty offerings, raise funds, and place graduates. Pilot projects will be conducted prior to the gradual implementation of these reforms.

Reform in Postgraduate Education. Postgraduate training programs and the degree system will be improved. Pilot projects will be launched to revise the regulations governing an institution's authorization to confer master's degrees and the qualifications of a professor wishing to take doctoral degree candidates. Furthermore, the system of quality control and evaluation will be strengthened. In addition to training teachers and scientific researchers, such programs will undertake major efforts to train qualified personnel with applied knowledge for economic and social development. Outstanding employees who have practical experience will be encouraged to study for advanced degrees through various channels. During this period of study, these employees will engage in teaching, research, and management. School authorities will determine their wages, based on management system innovations, personal work performance, and the wage scale for staff.

Reform in Specialized Secondary Schools. In the spirit of reforming higher education, corresponding reforms in specialized secondary schools will be undertaken. In accordance with relevant state policies, local governments and competent departments will offer joint-venture education, sponsored training, or self-supported learning. Students may be employed in either urban or rural work units in the government or private sector. Primary policies will be formulated by the central government; local governments will be responsible for devising overall plans and providing guidance.

Reform in Personnel Policies. The internal management of higher education institutions will be restructured to emphasize personnel system modifications. In order to determine the appropriate number of employees, a position responsibility system and contract system for teachers and staff will be established, with remuneration varying according to work performance. This reform measure is designed to promote egalitarianism, encourage enthusiasm for work, change the internal operational mechanisms of schools, improve school operation, and raise efficiency in higher education through policy guidance, ideological education, and material incentives.

The granting of professional titles and appointing professional personnel also will be revamped. The granting of professional titles will be based not only on academic standards but also on research, teaching proficiency, and practical application of research findings. University teachers will be employed using a contract system. Secondary and primary school teachers will be appointed by a system of qualifications tied to their instructional levels.

A system of assessing and appointing college graduates for employment will be initiated. Equal importance will be attached to school records, diplomas, certificates of technical competence, and other such certificates to dissuade accentuating degrees solely from institutions of higher learning.

Establishing salary grades will promote change in the education system. On the basis of working competency and performance, salaries of university and secondary technical school graduates will be divided into grades by employers. Also, local governments will formulate policies on allowances and monetary rewards to encourage graduates from assorted schools and disciplines to work in rural and remote areas or shoulder less-desirable occupations.

Reform in Management of Education. Policy guidance will be improved and school management intensified. The principle of stressing both ability and political integrity will be adhered to in enrolling students, employing graduates, rewarding and recognizing outstanding personnel, determining teachers' professional titles, recruiting teachers, raising teachers' salaries, and sending teachers and prospective teachers to study abroad. The performance of teachers in teaching ethics and in participating in practical work in society will be considered to be just as important as their performance in teaching.

School rules and regulations will be strictly followed, and students will be urged to observe proper norms of conduct, so as to develop a healthy and lively campus culture, to create an excellent school atmosphere, to encourage all students to study diligently, and to turn schools into centers for advancing socialist culture and ideology.

The philosophy of education will be further reformed and teaching curriculum and methodologies improved to prevent school education from being divorced from the needs of economic and social development. Curricula will be updated and revised in accordance with the latest advances in modern science, technology, and culture and in light of the actual needs of the socialist modernization drive. Training in basic knowledge, theories, and skills will be strengthened, with stress on the need to enhance the students' ability to analyze and solve problems and to train talented students. Concrete measures will be taken to lighten the heavy burden of study on students.

TVE schools will emphasize fostering occupational ethics and practical abilities among students. The range of specialties available in higher education will be expanded, and teaching will be more integrated with practical work and training. Institutions of higher education will strengthen cooperation with work units in society in carrying out training, so as to combine teaching with research and production.

Quality standards and indicators will be set for evaluating schools in all categories. Local departments of education will regularly assess the quality of instruction in schools. The number of school supervisors will increase and the supervising system will be improved. For technical, vocational, and higher education, assessment and evaluation will be conducted by school cadres, experts, and employers. Employers also will evaluate graduates and report to the graduating institution.

School textbooks will reflect the cultural advances of China and other countries and the latest developments in contemporary science and technology. A variety of primary and secondary level textbooks will be published, so long as their basics are the same. Local departments of education will be encouraged to compile textbooks suited to rural primary and secondary schools. Technical and vocational schools will compile a comprehensive set of teaching materials. As the variety of textbooks for higher education increases, their quality will be improved so as to better integrate theory with practice and combine socialist ideology with scientific knowledge.

Physical and hygiene education will be emphasized in all sectors of society, including education for parents, who will be encouraged to promote their children's fitness and well-being. Governments at all levels will create the necessary conditions to provide teachers, funds, sports grounds, and other facilities so that physical education can be offered successfully.

National defense and its relevance will receive more attention. Students in institutions of higher learning, secondary specialized schools, and senior secondary schools will receive more and varied military training. Education and military affairs departments will coordinate their efforts to implement such training.

Because art education fosters one's aesthetic concepts and abilities and develops moral integrity, the importance of aesthetics will be enhanced. New subjects and majors will be added to the curriculum, art education exchange programs will be expanded, and teaching strategies will be improved at all levels.

Physical labor will be stressed and labor skills taught. All schools will incorporate physical work into their instructional plans. Business communities will participate by extending the use of their work sites for such purposes.

Society as a whole will support the well-being of children and young people. Education outside the classroom, including education at home, will be linked to school education. Parents will be responsible to society and to their children. They will use "correct" methods for raising their children, developing sound moral standards and conduct. The departments in charge of the press and publishing, radio and television, and culture and art will provide a rich variety of intellectual products conducive to the healthy development of youth. In urban areas, more science centers, museums, libraries, gymnasiums, and youth centers will be constructed. A system for providing student access to public cultural facilities, either free or at a discount rate, will be established. Governments at all levels will implement the Law on the

Protection of Minors and employ severe measures to ban and eliminate pornographic books, magazines, and audiovisual products. Violators will be prosecuted to the fullest extent of the law.

As strengthening the Communist Party is the most fundamental guarantee for executing new education policies, promoting reform, and improving the quality of education, the party will continue to exercise leadership over schools. Party organizations in the schools will put into practice the spirit of the Fourteenth National Party Congress; will teach all party members, teachers, staff members, and students the theory of building socialism with Chinese characteristics; and will study the major issues in school reform.

Party members will set a good example, maintain close ties with the masses, and encourage people to promote the reform. In institutions of higher learning in which the president assumes leadership under the direction of the party committees, the committees will settle major issues through discussion, but administrative leaders will be guaranteed their rights. In primary, secondary, and other schools where the principal responsibility system is instituted, the party organization will be the political nucleus.

Reform of Teacher Education

Chinese leaders believe that education is the best hope for revitalizing the Chinese nation and that the hope for revitalizing education abides in the teachers. Since the end of the Cultural Revolution, the Chinese government has stressed the important role of teacher education and has endeavored to improve the social status of teachers. Government mandates have reiterated the vital role of teacher education, both preservice and inservice, in the development of nine-year compulsory education.

Training a relatively stable contingent of teachers of varying ages who have sound political integrity and professional skills is the key to reform and the development of education in China. Education reform sets new and more stringent demands for teachers. "As the engineers of human souls, they must work hard to improve their political integrity and professional competence; they must cherish the cause of education, foster qualified personnel through their teaching, and be worthy of the name of teachers" (Central Committee and the State Council 1993, p. 3).

The new educators are expected to organize their teaching, participate in education reform, and continually improve the quality of their instruction. Consequently, various policies and measures have been adopted to elevate teachers' social status; improve their working, studying, and living conditions; and enhance their teaching skills

In September 1992 the State Commission of Education drafted and distributed the document, *Basic Requirement for the Training of the Professional Skills Required of Students Enrolled in Tertiary Teacher Training Institutions.* Skills required include mastery of Putonghua (standard spoken Chinese), competence in verbal and written expression, mastery of the three penmanships, proper use of instruction strategies, and application of student advisement techniques.

The basic requirements for mastery of Putonghua and verbal and written expression are accuracy in speaking Putonghua at or near the second-level standard of "Proficiency in Putonghua" (as designated by the National Committee of Chinese Language), ability to read and communicate, and command of various verbal skills needed in classroom instruction.

The three penmanships consist of standard chalk, fountain pen, and Chinese pen or brush. Proficiency requirements are mastery of figures, structure, strokes, and the stroke order of the 3,755 characters of the primary level; mastery of regular script and running-hand style of the three penmanships; correct use and writing of punctuation; and competence in practical composition.

Instruction strategies include unit and lesson planning; lesson presentation skills; interpersonal communication skills, including use of the blackboard in classroom instruction; evaluation and assessment techniques; use of audiovisual equipment (slides, projectors, television, and other instructional media); organization and supervision of extracurricular activities; and application of pedagogical and psychological knowledge to conduct instructional research.

Student advisement techniques include organizing the class collective; directing class meetings, Youth League, and Young Pioneer activities; managing extracurricular, social practice, and other collective activities both in and out of school; training in either music, gymnastics, or art; applying principles of child psychology; and training students to comply with daily behavior standards.

In order to enhance the quality of instruction in specialized secondary schools or normal schools that train primary school teachers, the Normal School Department of the State Commission of Education convened a normal school syllabus committee comprised of editors from the People's Educational Publishing House, university professors, and teachers of secondary education institutions. In September 1992, the State Commission approved and released the committee's program of studies. Prospective primary teachers soon will be required to take the following courses: ideological politics, Chinese, math, physics, chemistry, biology, history, geography, educational psychology, pedagogy of elementary education, music, physical education, arts, and labor skills.

Since teacher education is designed to train qualified primary and secondary teachers, governments at all levels will increase their investment in education and will offer more training. Outstanding secondary school graduates will be encouraged to take the entrance examinations for teachers colleges and schools. An obligatory service period for graduates will ensure that they teach in primary and secondary schools. Other institutions of higher learning will play a role in training teachers for primary, secondary, and technical-vocational schools.

To enhance the skills of seasoned primary and secondary school teachers, policies will encourage middle-aged teachers to pursue advanced studies. By increasing the number of teachers and providing on-the-job training, the government projects that by the year 2000 most primary and secondary teachers will have earned diplomas or academic equivalency certificates. Also, the proportion of primary and junior secondary school teachers who are graduates from institutions of higher education will be increased.

College teachers will be trained on the job, with an emphasis on learning-by-doing supplemented by a variety of other approaches. Institutions of higher learning that employ numerous faculty and research staff will play a key role in training teachers. University/school partnerships will encourage ties between teachers and society. Working in their fields of expertise, senior experts will be invited to teach in the schools. Exchanges of college teachers also will be promoted. Finally, young and middle-aged teachers will be trained to form the mainstay of teachers and researchers.

Wage and Status Reform. Revamping the wage system includes gradually increasing teachers' wages and material benefits until they reach the level of the same category of personnel working in state-owned enterprises. By the year 2000 the average salary will exceed that of employees working in local state-owned enterprises. The average salary will fall in the middle to high ranks of the 12 sectors of the national economy. The salary of college teachers also will exceed that of employees working in state-owned enterprises.

A mechanism for regular salary increases suited to the characteristics of education will guarantee that salary levels parallel the gradual growth of the gross national product. The principle of distribution according to work will be administered. The practice of determining compensation and promotion strictly by seniority will be overturned. Teachers demonstrating meritorious contributions or excellent teaching performance will receive higher pay. The wage system formerly controlled by the central authorities will be revised so that local governments, departments of education, and schools will resolve salary matters under the macro-control of the state. The state will formulate the basic guidelines and structure of the wage system. Salary levels of province, autonomous regions, and municipalities directly under the central government will be set by special departments. Salaries will not be lower than the basic salary amounts of central government workers. The practice of universal salary, a uniform salary countrywide, will be eliminated. Schools will have the right to modify the salary structure, increase wages, and distribute school funds as they see fit.

To meet the needs of the 21st century, a contingent of teachers who are capable, qualified, and well-compensated is essential. To increase efficiency, the administration and staff of schools will be streamlined. Balanced standards for the size of school staff will be set; current staffing will be reduced, while the proportion of teachers to students will be increased. Departments of personnel, labor, and education, as well as the schools themselves, will help redundant staff find jobs according to their professional competence and abilities under the state plan.

Teachers will receive preferential treatment and priority in housing and other benefits. All levels of government will draft plans to increase the average living space per person of school personnel to that of the average level of the local inhabitants as soon as possible. As housing is gradually put on a commercial basis, school teachers and other staff will have priority in terms of construction, distribution, selling, or renting of housing. Local governments and departments that are responsible for housing construction for educators will explore a variety of channels to raise the funds for this purpose. Local governments and departments also will increase investment in housing construction for school personnel. In addition to improving housing conditions, medical care systems, retirement pension systems, and other forms of social insurance will be established for teachers in all areas.

Regulations to honor either the collective or individuals exhibiting meritorious teaching or research will be promulgated. All levels of schools, academic bodies, social organizations, teachers, and individuals will be eligible to apply for Teaching Achievement Awards. Three awards will be available — special, first, and second — and will provide certificates, medals, or money. The criteria and amounts allotted will be determined by the governments of provinces, autonomous regions, and municipalities. Governments, business enterprises, and individuals will be encouraged to contribute funds for awards to deserving teachers.

Efforts to improve the situation among Minban teachers (teachers teaching in a civilian school whose salaries are paid by the local community) will be increased. For historical reasons, many such teachers exist in rural areas. Local authorities will improve the management system for salaries of Minban teachers and will devise overall plans for increasing their subsidies and material benefits so that they enjoy the same salaries and benefits as Gongban teachers (teachers working in public schools that are supported by the government). Living allowances will be provided to retired Minban teachers, and insurance and pension funds gradually will be established. Teachers colleges and schools will select students from among Minban teachers for further training on a precondition enrollment basis. In light of actual conditions, each year local authorities will allot a number of Gongban teaching posts to outstanding Minban educators. In this way, the number of Minban teachers will gradually be reduced.

Solving the Problem of Unqualified Teachers. Unqualified teachers constitute a large percentage of the teacher population, and the majority of teachers in the rural areas are unable to "come out, or pass the entrance examination or stick it out once enrolled" ("Speeding Up the Pace," p. 208). Therefore, the State Commission of Education in 1992 released the document, *Suggestions on Enhancing the Pace of Training for the Acquisition of Formal Qualifications for Secondary School Teachers Not Fully Qualified.* This document recommends that a new teacher training model be established that integrates correspondence education, satellite television education, and a self-study qualifications exam. The model will adopt a unified curriculum, teaching plan, and teaching textbooks in which participating junior middle school teachers will learn what they will teach. Enrollment will be limited to those who pass the unified entrance examination.

During such training, the teachers will earn qualifications by means of tests on a subject-by-subject basis. If they fail one test, the model provides for make-up tests. The unified qualification tests will be created at the provincial level under the leadership of the provincial commission of education. These tests will be administered by the provincial normal institutes or provincial normal university. Special training classes, considered training institutes, will be offered in the normal schools at the district level. (A district usually includes about five counties.) The normal university that writes the qualification tests will not be allowed to conduct the training programs. On the completion of all the required courses and the passing of all qualification tests, the participants of the integrated training program will be awarded the appropriate diploma.

Constructing the Normal Schools. In November 1992 more than 150 representatives from 20 provinces attended a national symposium on accelerating the construction of normal schools. The symposium summarized changes in normal schools over the last few years. Achievements cited included improved school conditions as facilities and faculty composition met the minimum requirements set by the government; operating schools to serve the basic education goals, actively adjusting to the changing demand for labor and coping with the need for better teacher education as a result of the junior middle school education reform; reforming the core curriculum and raising the overall quality of normal school education; and adhering to the socialist orientation, attaching importance to the school moral educational work, and improving and strengthening the ideological education of the students.

The symposium participants visited five normal schools in Jiangsu Province and rated them highly. All of these schools adhered to the socialist orientation in school operation and to the guiding thought of promoting nine-year compulsory education, supporting research in normal school training programs, promoting teachers' basic skill training, stressing practice based on internships, effective school administration, and a positive atmosphere for learning.

Participants further agreed that five former concepts required replacement: 1) education serving the planned economy should give way to a model of education serving the socialist market economy; 2) the closed uniformed school model should be transformed to a new model in which the main task of the school is to serve basic education, or nine-year compulsory education; 3) government as the sole funding source for education should be changed to a system in which the government is the main financial source but additional funding is welcomed — and expected — from other channels; 4) the concept that the normal school is a pure educational institute should be altered to recognize that the normal school can run enterprises and be engaged in technological development; and 5) the old concept of middle school education that is examination-driven should be discarded in favor of middle school education that is quality-driven.

CONCLUSION

Looking at education in China in the past, at today's education realities in the People's Republic, and at China's plans for the future, one can readily see that education always has been in the spotlight — albeit dimmer at some times and brighter at other times. Education at all levels will continue to be a focal point in government planning both in and for the future.

Perhaps this past-present-future perspective on Chinese education — in particular, teacher education — can best be summed up by the words of one official. In 1985, the Deputy State Education Commissioner, He Dong-chang, described the future of China's teacher education as follows:

> In approximately 15 years a qualified, stable, and sufficient teaching force for kindergartens, primary schools, and secondary schools will be fostered through persistent efforts. These prospective teachers will be required to possess a strong sense of mission as educators. They are to be dedicated, well educated, and highly moral, possessing solid academic background, sound physical constitution, and competency in teaching. To achieve this objective, three phases of development are planned: Phase 1: For the first 5-7 years (1985-1992), the emphasis will be on the training and reorganization of the existing in-service teaching force, making most teachers competent in their teaching. At the same time, close attention will be paid to providing teachers for subjects for which there is an exceptionally severe shortage. Phase 2: In the next 5-7 years (1992-1999), further replenishment and cultivation of teachers for all subjects will be stressed. Most of the teachers will be required to be fully competent in teaching and well prepared in their subject-matter areas. Phase 3: Finally, based on the implementation of 9-year compulsory education, great efforts will be

made to foster a teaching force which meets a high standard of academic and professional preparation. Thus by the early part of the 21st century, China will have an improved system of education for teachers and be able to train sufficient numbers of well qualified teachers for its vast system of education. (Yang et al. 1989, p. 111)

The Chinese government and Chinese educators appear to be adhering to the established guidelines and are working diligently to achieve the stated goals and objectives.

The People's Republic of China has been rightly called "a sleeping giant." Most observers agree that the giant is waking up. Chinese education is responding to that awakening.

REFERENCES

Brauchli, M.W. "Class Issue: Wary of Education but Needing Brains, China Faces a Dilemma." *Wall Street Journal*, 15 November 1994, pp. A1, A5.

Central Committee of the Communist Party of China and the State Council. "Outline for Reform and Development of Education in China." *Renmin Ribao* [People's Daily], 27 February 1993, pp. 1-3.

Chen, C., and Uttal, D.H. "Cultural Values, Parents' Beliefs, and Children's Achievement in the United States and China." *Human Development* 31, no. 6 (1988): 351-58.

Creel, H.G. *Chinese Thought from Confucius to Mao Tse-tung*. New York: New American Library, 1953.

Deng X. *Selected Works of Deng Xiaoping (1975-1980)*. Beijing: People's Publishing House, 1983.

Department of Planning and Construction. *Educational Statistics Yearbook of China, 1994*. Beijing: People's Education Press, 1994.

Dong, C. "On the Reform of Basic Education in China." In *China Educational Sciences*, by the editors of the Central Institute of Educational Research. Beijing: Educational Sciences Publishing House, 1988.

"First Grade, First Semester Chinese." In *Text for Nine-Year Compulsory Education*. Shanghai: Shanghai Education Publishing House, 1993.

Hawkins, J.N., and Stites, R. "Strengthening the Future's Foundation: Elementary Education Reform in the People's Republic of China." *Elementary School Journal* 92, no. 1 (1991): 43-60.

Huang, L.J. "The Chinese-American Family." In *Ethnic Families in America: Patterns and Variations*, edited by C.H. Mindel and R.W. Habenstein. New York: Elsevier Scientific Publishing, 1976.

Information Office of the State Council of the People's Republic of China. *The Progress of Human Rights in China*. Beijing, 1995.

Kuo, P.W. *The Chinese System of Public Education*. New York: Steinman and Foltz, 1915.

Liu Z. *Collection of Liu Zhongyuan's Works: Vol. 19. On Teacher*. Beijing: China Book Bureau, 1979.

Po, W.W. "A Crisis in the 'Hundred Year Tree of Education'." *Inside China Mainland* 15 (July 1993): 63.

"Speeding Up the Pace of Training for the Acquisition of Formal Qualifications for Secondary School Teachers Not Fully Qualified." In *China Education Yearbook, 1993*. Beijing: People's Education Press, 1994.

State Education Commission, People's Republic of China (SEDC). *Education in China*. Beijing, 1989.

State Education Commission, People's Republic of China (SEDC). *Chinese Education at a Glance: Essential Statistics for 1992*. Beijing, 1993.

Stevenson, H.W. "Learning from Asian Schools." *Scientific American* 267 (December 1992): 32-38.

Stevenson, H.W.; Lee, S.Y.; Chen, C.; Lummis, M.; Stigler, J.; Fan, L.; and Ge, F. "Mathematics Achievement of Children in China and the United States." *Child Development* 61, no. 4 (1990): 1053-1066.

Sun P. *History of Chinese Education*. Shanghai: Eastern China Normal University Press, 1993.

Text for Nine-Year Compulsory Education. Shanghai: Shanghai Education Publishing House, 1993.

Triandis, H.C.; Brislin, R.; and Hui, C.H. "Cross-Cultural Training Across the Individualism-Collectivism Divide." *International Journal of Intercultural Relations* 12, no. 3 (1988): 269-89.

Yang, Z.L.; Lin, B.; and Su, W.C. *Teacher Education in the People's Republic of China*. Beijing: Beijing Normal University Press, 1989.

ABOUT THE AUTHORS

Rhea A. Ashmore is a professor of literacy studies in the School of Education at the University of Montana. She is a former exchange scholar to Shanghai International Studies University, where she taught in the English Department. Ashmore holds four earned university degrees, including a Doctor of Education in curriculum and instruction from the University of Montana, which she received in 1981.

Zhen Cao is a visiting instructor in the College of Arts and Sciences at the University of Montana. A former lecturer in English at Shanghai International Studies University, he left the People's Republic of China in 1989 to earn his Doctor of Education in education administration, which he received from the University of Montana in 1996.